Diary of a Ghetto Priest

Diary of a Ghetto Priest

Prayers + Blessings
Fr Ho Lung MOP

FR. RICHARD HO LUNG, M.O.P.

Missionaries of the Poor Kingston

Cover Photograph: Missionaries of the Poor
Missionaries of the Poor
PO Box 29893
Atlanta, GA 30359
www.MissionariesofthePoor.org

Cover design by David Ferris, www.DavidFerrisDesign.com

Cataloging-in-Publication data on file with the Library of Congress.

ISBN 978-1-505108-38-5

CONTENTS

FOREWORD

GRACED with great faith and a vision of life with Christ among the poor, Fr. Richard Ho Lung heads Missionaries of the Poor, a religious community of men in the Roman Catholic Church. Founded in Jamaica in 1981 and then called Brothers of the Poor, the community has been guided by Fr. Ho Lung with his deeply contemplative spirituality and his considerable gifts, talents, and tenacity. The community has grown to include over 550 men and continues to attract more members.

Bound under vows of chastity, poverty, obedience, and free service to the poor, the Brothers live a strict, disciplined, simple—some would say medieval!—life: living in a cloistered community with common dormitories, wearing flowing cassocks with plain crosses around their necks, possessing as individuals neither money nor goods, washing their own clothes, eating simply, with water as their daily drink. Their day begins at five-thirty in the morning and ends at ten at night. They have breakfast in silence and spend three and a half hours daily in prayer.

Anachronistic in today's secular, post-Christian world? No! These men, whose average age is twenty-four years, are more like stars that shine brightly wherever there is darkness, giving witness in their lives that God is not dead: God is alive! Out of their lives of discipline, prayer, and love of God and the poor as Christ, they leave their cloister to work and to be among the poor. The work is hands-on, serious, difficult, and demanding. Yet such is their love of Christ and the poor that they work with vibrancy, joy, and peace.

And such is the fullness of this life in the Spirit that the community now stretches around the world with missions in Jamaica, Haiti, India, the Philippines, Africa, Indonesia, East Timor, and North Carolina, USA. There are ministries to lepers, poor village children and entire families, homeless poor who are terminally ill with AIDS, physically and mentally disabled poor infants and children and young adults, indeed all God's children of any age or condition who are destitute and in need.

In an age when Christianity so often seems irrelevant, the Missionaries of the Poor give living witness to the profound relevancy of Christianity when it is lived out and given flesh with Christ and his poor at the centre of life.

Grace Washington

INTRODUCTION

T WELVE years ago I realized I must give witness to the incredible discoveries I had made among the poor. Thus I told the message in *The Daily Gleaner*, the leading newspaper in our island, in a series of entries called "Diary of a Ghetto Priest."

Working in the ghetto, I had gotten to the heart of Christ's love for the poor. One would think that he served them out of a sense of duty, requiring heroic self-denial and offering no pleasure. But I learned that he loved them because they are lovable: there is much extraordinary beauty in the least of our brothers and sisters. They possess such undying hope, such rootedness in basic human reality, passions, and experiences, such dignity, such sense of honour, such love of life and of God.

The intellectual life can be much spinning in mud and the Christian so separated from existential faith. The poor saved me from a mental life of boredom and a safe Christianity without the flesh and blood of Christ. The poor actually require the deepest thought, hard labour, contemplation, and a bold and deep leap into God's call to death and rebirth. In addition, the poor are most charming, rich and complex in their blend of opposite qualities: good and evil, light and dark, love and hate. They cannot and do not live a logical and predictable life. They are devoid of anything stable or anyone stable in life. And, having nothing, they invent ways of living, cause for laughter, and

1

dig deep into the depths of their souls for God, for meaning, for love, for truth. In everyday life they cry out, they laugh, they plunge recklessly and grasp hungrily for the ephemeral gift of God they sense in the miracle of everyday life. They give thanks that somehow there is a bit of food and clothes to wear for yet another day.

In the poor I found Christ's life palpably present. In their lives I saw incarnated the battle between God and the devil. The poor often yield to temptation—lies, theft, promiscuity, drugs, violence—but they hate it and know the indignity to their persons for having blundered. And having blundered they seek for the Lord and His forgiveness again and again. There is also warmth among the poor; always there is a welcome, a song, a prayer in this dark ghetto world wrought by neglect, injustice, selfishness, and exploitation.

Thank God for those young men, Fr. Brian Kerr and Fr. Hayden Augustine, who offered their lives to Christ and journeyed with me in faith into the world of Jesus of Nazareth and his poor. Thank God for our early religious brothers, Murray Goodman and Maximo Medina, who bore on their shoulders the heavy Cross of the homeless and destitute. They have worked tirelessly night and day to make real the daily works of Jesus. Archbishop Emeritus Samuel Carter, our beloved Ordinary, encouraged us way past duty. He was a father to us, grumpy sometimes, but always encouraging us with his huge magnanimous heart. Thank God mostly for Christ and his Gospel message. He gave meaning to our lives in the beatitudes, defining for us what is happiness and the true meaning of life. Because of him we were able to see the kingdom of God in the ghetto.

Chapter One

....

"The kingdom of heaven is like a merchant in search of fine pearls, who, on finding one pearl of great value, went and sold all that he had and bought it."

Mt 13:45-56

IN the beginning, I did this work because I had to. It was a matter of conscience. God requires much from his followers. Not only was I a Christian but also a priest. I could not be a priest and not work among the poor—not after having seen the hunger, the nakedness, the anger, and worst of all the terrifying homelessness of many of our people who call Jamaica home.

I had lectured much to students at the university and high schools. My purpose was to move future leaders with the word that they might serve God and our people, in particular the poor. But words are empty without action. How could I tell others to work with the poor without myself doing it? My words were disembodied from my actions. Day after day I brought myself to the classroom or to the Church but hardly to the poor.

"The word was made flesh and dwelt among us." What mysterious words! I understood them to mean that my words required the reality. If I said we must work with the poor, my flesh must be brought also among them. Christ was among the poor first and foremost. He was God in the flesh among the poor. So too, if I was to follow in his footsteps, I had to be among the poor.

3

We are told by Christ himself in the Gospel of Matthew, "As you did it to the least of these my brethren, you did it to me." This means Christ and the poor are interchangeable. He is the poor, and the poor are Christ. Jesus is now gone, but in the poor we find Christ today.

I hated the stench of faeces: I hated the nakedness, the hunger, the ugliness, the anger, the weeping. But I went among the poor because Christ commanded it. Then I did not have the vision. I did not truly see Christ disguised in the poor. I worked grimly and without humour until I understood that Christ wanted me to be with the poor not to change the world of the poor materially, but to be among them and to find Christ's beauty among them.

Yes, there are clothes, water, food, shelter, money that we give. We give all that we can. We beg mightily, and we work fully to bring our poor some material comfort; but most importantly, it is the beauty we discover among the poor, the presence of Christ that holds us there. Love means being with those whom we love. Just as God loved us by being with us in the flesh of His son, we find Christ by being with the poor in whom he dwells.

Learning to laugh also helped. Laughter is the butterfly in the garden of the poor. The light of hope pulls us forward, and joy is our reaction to having found hope. Among the poor, we live and discover epiphanies of Christ. We are driven by a divine impulse to give hope to others, while we ourselves find meaning and fulfil our hope of being truly Christian. It is spirit pulsating in our blood and veins.

The scales fall from our eyes. As mature Christians we find beauty in ugliness, and we see riches in poverty. The sadness of being Christians without Christ passes away. The Cross so grotesque and repugnant reveals itself as the only thing of beauty:

it is light, not darkness, it is life-giving, not emptiness. Work with the poor is God's love for man. The poor: they are beautiful, they are the kingdom of God, the pearl discovered which we must purchase at all cost. Among the poor we discover true meaning—Christ himself, our beloved whom we require and for whom the soul hungers. Without him, we languish and die.

Once I worked with the poor because I had to; it was commanded by the Lord. Today I work among the poor because I will, for among them I have discovered the kingdom—the riches of the spiritual life and the beauty of the Cross—which gives me more than I could ever give, the gift of hope.

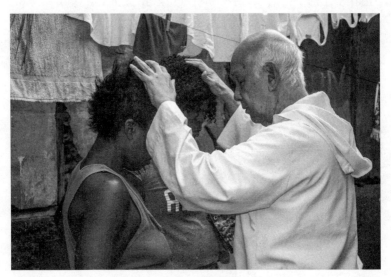
Blessed are the poor, for theirs is the kingdom of God.

Chapter Two

*"For truly I say to you, if you have faith as a grain
of mustard seed, you will say to this mountain, 'Move
hence to yonder place', and it will move; and nothing
will be impossible to you."*

Mt 17:20

"YOU are condemning this country," the Minister of
Local Government told me. "I demand that you withdraw the books you sent overseas." The reporters he had called
in and I were shocked.

"I will not withdraw it."

"If you will not, the Prime Minister will deal with you
himself."

"I will not withdraw it."

We had distributed the book of pictures of Eventide residents to raise funds. We wanted to replace the condemned
building burnt down in the fire that killed a hundred and fifty
old women. It showed the truth of Eventide, contrary to the
beauty and prosperity the government wanted to project overseas. Rats had attacked the children at Eventide and bitten their
lips and ear lobes. Rats had also attacked two old people; one
old lady had a heart attack. We were angry and called a friend.
He was disturbed and called *The Star*. Phyllis Thomas was
brave enough to cover the story.

The Minister of Local Government was concerned that the
public locally and overseas would know about the poverty, sickness, and death at Eventide. But to pretend prosperity, which

exists for only a small percentage of our people, is makeup plastered on the face of a corpse.

Decade after decade had come and gone, and no government had enough love for the people at Eventide to relieve their suffering, sadness, and death. We had had enough waiting: the more than five hundred people at Eventide symbolized for us the helplessness of the poor. The people had hardly any food. Many old people lay in their shame in rags or naked and exposed. We saw children stark raving mad. One boy I remember well used to eat his faeces. Others used to wander out of the wards and were bitten by pigs in the yard. The workers were demoralized. Death itself seemed to have taken permanent residence at Eventide, and nobody from government reacted to what was happening.

No, I would not withdraw those books. The truth is consecrated: it is absolute; it is divine. I believe that. He who speaks the truth speaks the words of God. If one had to lie or hide the truth to promote tourism, I would not. God was strong in my heart. Jesus Christ himself would have cursed the government for the lies they would have me perpetrate by denying the evils at Eventide for the benefit of tourism. If the work of the government is the economy, the work of Christians is to bring justice.

Then God intervened. I watched in wonderment as He orchestrated liberation of our poor and oppressed at Eventide. The members of the press present at the confrontation by the Minister of Local Government reported the whole matter. It got to the radio and television stations. Every voice was a drop swelling into a stream; voice upon voice converged on the public media and flooded into one thunderous voice swamping our land, thirsty for truth and justice.

During that period I was silent. I spoke to nobody from the press. I knew He was at work. God had penetrated the hearts of the people. Their voices were His voice. He desired that the least of our brethren be fed, clothed, and housed. The people, seized by God's grace and power, would not be denied.

The Prime Minister called Sammy Henriques and me. We were to head a committee to build a brand new home—the Golden Age Home. A friend had said, "Forget about Eventide. It can't be done." Being a businessman, he is pragmatic. But it had happened. Faith doesn't ask how; it doesn't rely on logic to effect changes. God overcame all with His will and the new home was built. Indeed, "All things are possible with God."

The mystery of death to resurrection had been enacted again. I have lived to witness this in my life. I was grateful and humbled that God had used me as an instrument to fulfil His will. And I, being nothing but a poor fool wanting to serve Him in my weakness and limitedness, can only wonder at the mystery of it all. I am nothing, yet He accomplished great things through me. Everyone had despaired: nobody had expected anything to be accomplished for the people at Eventide. But God had worked a miracle.

Our Brothers journey into a world of crime, poverty, and neglect, and yet there is joy.

Chapter Three

....

"When it was evening, there came a rich young man from Arimathea, named Joseph, who also was a disciple of Jesus. He went to Pilate and asked for the body of Jesus. Then Pilate ordered it to be given to him. And Joseph took the body, and wrapped it in a clean linen shroud, and laid it in his own new tomb, which he had hewn in the rock."

Mt 27:57-60a

FERDIE had made the journey into the unknown. Mr. Charlton had died at Eventide, but the image of that man covered with sores and dying coalesced with the image of Christ on the Cross.

Joe Charlton was covered with sores. He became Jesus for Ferdie and the Brothers. His skin was jet black, but big pink sores were all over him. His entire face, hands, legs—yes, even his belly and back—were covered with yellow pus and scabs. It was a miracle that out of this near corpse could come breath and a voice, "You pray for me, Father."

"Yes, Joe."

"And how is the day?" He couldn't tell because he was blind.

"It is beautiful."

"What you bring for me today?" he asked cheerfully.

"I have some milk and a half-bar of soap and toothpaste."

"That is useful and very kind of you."

I looked at the pathetic figure: the arms and legs paralyzed— stiff dried sticks—and the tall gaunt figure and the face with eyes gone blind and lips puffy. He was only fit for burial, and the maggots the Brothers cleaned had gotten a head start.

Ferdie stood beside him aghast and whispered, "Lord Jesus."

I took Joe's hand but with feelings of revulsion. His fingers curled and held onto my fingers. The warmth and love from his body flowed from his fingers into mine. I closed my other hand over his and didn't worry about the pus. And love warmed me through and through. This is the infusion of the Holy Spirit, and God's grace filling me with divine life.

We sat at the edge of his bed and prayed silently for a while. Then we said the Lord's Prayer. Afterwards, we talked. "Where is your family, Mr. Charlton? How did you end up at Eventide?"

"Cho, they are young. They have to get along with their lives."

"You speak well. You must have had a good job."

"But times change, Father. My wife died, and I had no reason to live. I drank and lost my job just before I was due pension. I didn't want to live any longer. But now I am ready for the Father,"

Ferdie, the Brothers, and I passed on to the other people in the ward. We wanted to say hello to as many people as possible.

"Thank you for visiting, Father, Mr. Mahfood."

"Thank you, Mr. Charlton, for having us visit you." And silently, I thanked him for bringing Christ to me.

That night Ferdie said he prayed all night long. How could he live in Jamaica all his life and not know what was happening. Mr. Charlton was like an emblem marked permanently on his mind. Truly his flesh was rotten. Indeed, he was a worm and no man. Yet, Mr. Charlton maintained his dignity. The cruelty of neglect, the sins of omission against the poor agonized Ferdie. He knelt and wept and begged the Lord to forgive him.

How can we pursue our ambitions while men and women—Jesus' own sisters and brothers—die in our island, broken, despised, and forgotten? It is not right. God does not will it. We must clothe the naked, comfort the afflicted, feed the hungry. That day Ferdie and I walked away friends. We had shared as brothers the broken body of Christ in Mr. Charlton.

Hello darling Rose, ghetto mother of the poor.

Chapter Four

....

"Comfort, comfort my people,
says your God.
Speak tenderly to Jerusalem
and cry to her
that her warfare is ended,
that her iniquity is pardoned,
that she has received from the Lord's
hand double for all her sins."

Is 40:1-2

LENA is quite a lady. Her mind is so acute, and her beauty so dignified. This is in spite of her skeleton body propped up on the worn walking stick. She is blind and behind dark glasses.

"Lena, how do you like your new home?"

"I like it, Father. Though I gave you a hard time."

"You're glad we took you away?"

"Eventide was a sewer. You get used to anything though."

"But you're glad you came?"

"Here is heaven."

I looked around Golden Age, the new home. It was worth the battles. Sir John Golding was just great, and our Jamaican government really cooperated in bringing all this about. There is a gentleness and sense of order surrounding this new home, and the people are content. God will bless our country for taking care of these homeless.

Lena told me about the time when the condemned building at Eventide burnt down. There were cracks in the floor and the walls. It could easily be blown over in a storm and with one match stick could go up.

"It was the blackest of nights when the fire circled the bottom floor and rose up in a high blaze to trap and swallow up all the people. Nobody know what was going on. It was sudden. Then the screams. If you ever see how people run like mad ants, and we fall on each other. I jump out of bed and cough till I nearly dead. Everything finish, everybody dead, except eight of we."

One hundred and fifty old women, their charred bodies looking like roasted pigs in a fire—a testimony to our irresponsibility and lack of awareness.

Lena spoke with me about the old days. When we first began our visits, we had nothing to give. We just visited. We were convinced if Jesus were alive today, the first place he would visit was Eventide. They were the most degraded—the blind, the lame, the deaf, the dumb, the retarded, the sick, the senile— God's chosen people. They had in common that they were hungry, homeless, and completely abandoned. Walking through Eventide in the heat of the sun, surrounded completely by the ghetto and hundreds of helpless people, was like walking the road to Calvary. And the result was always the same: the seriousness of our Lord's calling and the discovery of Christ crucified, forgotten and abandoned among the poor. Yes, indeed, these are his people. These are the little ones Jesus wants us to minister to. We were amongst the very ones Jesus was amongst. At Eventide, Brother Hayden, Brother Brian, and I found our true vocations in the poor people.

"Well, it's all over and done with. Praise the Lord," said Lena.

"No, Lena, Eventide is not over. Yesterday a baby was burnt in a fire on Foster Lane. Five children, the granny Maureen, and the daughter Precious spent the night cotching at the police station. Remember, Lena, that there was a waiting list of hundreds of homeless people trying to get into Eventide, living hell that it was. The people in the slums are like the people at Eventide; they, our brothers and sisters, could be condemned to death in a minute. Most buildings they live in are old, broken, and rotten, much like yours that burnt down."

There are houses on the hills of St. Andrew, the houses of people in high places, overlooking the massive slums down below. This island is still separated and divided. Who will take responsibility for the poor?

A lady offers food to the Brothers in the ghetto streets.

Chapter Five

....

"After a little while the bystanders came up and said to Peter, 'Certainly you are also one of them, for your accent betrays you.' Then he began to invoke a curse on himself and to swear, 'I do not know the man.' And immediately the cock crowed. And Peter remembered the saying of Jesus, 'Before the cock crows, you will deny me three times.' And he went out and wept bitterly."

Mt 26:73-75

ARE we just Sunday Christians, or are we followers of Christ?

The Cross! The Cross! No greater symbol of Christ's life on earth than the Cross. To lay down one's life for one's friends: that is where Christians draw the line.

"Oh, first and foremost, I must take care of myself and my children. Charity begins at home." But Christ's love is total otherness, welcoming the stranger, loving our enemies, doing good to those who hate us. The Cross is total. We either carry it, or we don't. If we do, we are Christians; if we don't, we are not.

Are we in Jamaica to get what we want, or are we here to love our people and to serve them—those dirty street people, helpless beggars, thieves, old people, alienated youth, illiterate children?

Tick tock, one o'clock. I know not the man.

Jamaica is a Christian country, so we say; yet there is so much hatred, violence, and poverty. Drive through St. Andrew

19

where there are people who surely can help, then into the slums where there is hunger, joblessness, violence. Christ must hang on the Cross between the rich and poor, bridging the people, forging them together through his life. The answer is not the pastor screaming in a microphone and the people trembling in mystical ecstasy, nor the pastor preaching cautiously to nodding parishioners decorated in white suits and black hats. Yes, Christianity has been betrayed in Jamaica.

Like Peter, we can remove ourselves and huddle by a fire seeking warmth and security rather than hanging in stark naked loneliness on Mount Calvary with our crucified Lord. Some of us gaze upon the Cross as if it were an icon or a marbled work of art to be admired, not hearing his words, "I thirst." We are Christians gone dead because of our selfishness and lack of concern.

Tick tock, two o'clock. I tell you, I know not the man.

The Cross! The Cross! Christ was wounded by mankind, not only by those who scoffed at him and spat on him and shoved nails in his hands, but by those who abandoned him and by his friends who weren't there. We Christians must not abandon the Cross. If we do, we abandon Christ and the true experience of Christianity. We must be bound to the wounds of Jesus, bound with him on the Cross. He tells us, "As you did it not to the least of these, you did it not to me." Christ judged people, not asking if they went to church but asking if they took the hungry, the naked, the prisoner unto themselves.

We must hold on to the flesh of broken humanity and offer tenderness and love. We must heal the wounds of broken mankind. We must kneel at the foot of the Cross and weep, for Christ has died. We sinners gambled and celebrated with wine while he drank the vinegar of human suffering.

We profess Christianity, but are we Christians? Our age is old. The materialism of our age has set in; people are trapped by the selfishness required to survive in our world. There is only one way to break out of the stranglehold. It is not by higher wages and greater production. It is by loving and sacrificing ourselves once again. In our time, Christians must be counter-cultural. Christians must live another way, not a life of materialism but of spirituality, not of power but of humility, not of indiscriminate sex but of purity, not of selfishness but of love.

Our times are old, they are dying.

Tick tock, three o'clock. He hangs stark naked on the rock of Mount Calvary. God is dead.

Beloved Brothers, God is love, and those who abide in God abide in love.

Chapter Six

....

"For he grew up before him like
a young plant,
and like a root out of dry ground;
he had no form or comeliness
that we should look at him,
and no beauty that we should desire him;
But he was wounded
for our transgressions,
he was bruised for our iniquities;
upon him was the chastisement
that made us whole,
and with his stripes we are healed."

Is 53:2, 5

T HE policeman had cradled in his lap a little boy child. It had cast eyes and very thin legs. The policeman was muscular but like a mother: it was an image of the biblical lion carrying in his arms the lamb.

"We don't know his name, Father. What will you call him?"

"Joel. The prophet."

The policeman laughed a hearty approval. He handed the boy over to our nurse Anne Marie as gently as could be.

"The mother, we believe, is from Sligoville. We can't find her. Joel is a twin child. The mother left off this child but has with her the other one. We might also have to bring the other to you."

Little Joel. What a sad little face! Both eyes are turned upwards towards the top of his head. He has a "bang" belly:

swollen with a big navel and stick-like arms and legs. Our nurse told me he is malnourished and full of worms. He is severely autistic and speaks not a word. He beats his head against the solid wall or against the floor. He seems partially paralyzed on the entire left side of his body, and drags his left leg when he walks. Always he has his left arm crooked as if it were hanging in a sling, and it is stiff with his fingers closed like a claw.

If I had to guess, Joel is four years old. He is not toilet trained, so he has to be led or lifted to the toilet. In his stool, I saw blood, due to internal bleeding we were to find out later. The blood was congealed in dark blotches. The policeman had said that the mother was known to beat Joel terribly.

Marvin, our little Down's syndrome boy, and Peter, a physically disabled but bright little boy, came up to Joel. They were quiet and gentle in their approach, but Joel shied away in a panic and hit at them. Joel never seems to smile and never looks anyone in the face. In fact, he likes to be left alone and often he returns to a corner in the dormitory or in the office and just continuously bashes his head against the desk or the wall. At other times, he finds himself a place in the blazing sun and lies down, curled up like a little butterfly, and sleeps. Beads of sweat pour out of him, but Joel does not move.

Peter and Marvin are fully alive with their lust for living although Peter is crippled and Marvin is not very intelligent. But they seem to know what is happening to Joel: that he needs his space, that they mustn't be too rough or too friendly, that Joel needs time to trust them and become part of the family.

Anne Marie has found a way of playing with him. She tickles him with a light touch. He laughs. She tickles him a little more. He giggles and gurgles. She tickles him a whole heap, and he laughs heartily. In Anne Marie, Joel has found a mother. Now he climbs into her lap and plays with her fingers and hugs her warmly. He is like a little butterfly slowly unfolding in the warmth of her motherly love.

Motherhood. In a time when modern women are becoming like men—office-bound, businesslike, efficient, and even hard—the children of our world will lose out. They will lose compassion, tenderness, and the intuitive powers of loving without reserve, without reason, without condition.

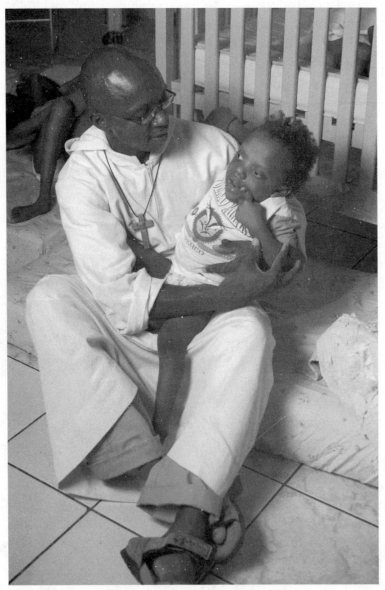

"Let the children come unto me." Many homeless and abandoned children are given to us all over the world.

Chapter Seven

*"For with thee is the fountain of life; in thy light
do we see light."*

Ps 36:9

ROHAN is a beautiful gift from the Lord. His mother came to the Lord's Place, our new home for the destitute, and delivered him to us in tears. Dressed in faded rags, torn and ill-fitting, she was not able to speak coherently. She had gone mad walking and begging on the streets, then sleeping on the sidewalks at night. Somehow in her madness, she saw with a clear vision that she could not take care of the child, and although she had the passionate feelings of a mother, it did not obscure the objective reality that her little one must survive in the care of someone else. She begged the Brothers to take care of the child. She said that she would not return as it would break her heart.

Rohan came to us suffering from severe and constant diarrhoea and dehydration. The Brothers took Rohan to Children's Hospital. The hospital authorities would not keep him since he would soon die. Moreover, in case he lingered on, a precious bed would be occupied for a long time. The Brothers tried another route. They brought Rohan to Dr. Palomino Lue. She gave her service free of charge and set about the medicines and diet needed to bring Rohan back to life.

That was three months ago. Rohan is now two and a half years old, a beautiful baby boy with a terrific smile. Yesterday when I held him in my arms, I could feel the warmth of his body against my legs and tummy. This was life, most precious and dear. He held on to my fingers, sucked my thumb, and looked on my face and smiled. I held him up in my arms, and a light sprang from his eyes, and I felt that the divine Christ child had smiled.

With each ounce of weight he added, we could see Rohan increase in energy. Each time we played with him, we could see that little light in his eyes increase. He was really beginning to enjoy life and to break out into sheer celebration of being alive. That precious gift given to each of us—life—that thing we hang onto, no matter what the struggles may be, was also his. Rohan kicks, laughs, and gurgles with delight when he enjoys food or companionship or pretty colours. He delights in just being alive in our world, as needy as he is as an orphan in our simple home.

Is this mere fancy on my part, or is it so, that little Rohan is the Christ child? I experienced Christ as real as Joseph holding Jesus in his arms. Rohan's life issues from the precious body of Christ who is the Alpha and Omega of our world. Rohan derives his life from Jesus, and he presents to me the beauty and tenderness and magnificence of Jesus.

Yes, Rohan is God's gift to us. And Christ is in all our other sixty-two babies and children. They effuse the divine life of Jesus to all of us.

At Christmas, you too can be Christ for them as they are for us. You too can be the love of God for our poor: praying for them, visiting them, and helping us to help them. Maybe one of you might also come forward and take Rohan in your arms and into your home, and then you will have Jesus in your arms on Christmas day.

Chapter Eight

....

"Let her glean even among the sheaves and do not reproach her."

Ruth 2:15

CLAUDETTE'S years of childbearing were hard labour. Fifteen years of almost continuous pregnancies and child labour would wear a body down to death. But Claudette grew stronger; her thin body was bony but not pitiful. She walked tall and straight, and her joy was a perennial flower that blossomed in her eyes with smiles for everyone to delight in. In all her suffering, why this joy? Her secret was a profound sense of life and her acceptance of it; the sweetness and bitterness all formed one reality. And she had a penetrating belief that the Cross is a sign of conquest.

She died each time she heard that she was pregnant. But soon the feeling of movement in her body would awaken a sense of being privileged. The growth of that living being within her, the swelling of her flesh day by day, the baby kicking, breathing, then making its passageway into the world were like a flame of living love. Claudette enjoyed bringing into the world a newborn babe.

This second man of hers, Errol, had given her seven children. She never married him; she swore she would never marry again. Errol did not sleep with her in the same house, but she took care of him. Each day she would prepare dinner for him, and she would warm his heart with her marvellous energy and

29

sense of victory at the end of each day, though brutally difficult and completely demanding.

"No, I will not marry you, Errol. I like to know where I stand. Any day you could walk out on me. If I have to do everything myself, then I am certain. I know I have to do everything, so I plan; then with the grace of God and hard labour, I provide."

Claudette's children were never allowed to beg. She would not allow them. When she was not at home, the children would play truant from school here and there, but not enough to be expelled. And Claudette commanded the children to save everything. She took it as a rule never to borrow. "Is like trading the present for the future. It can't work."

Her children had children, but they did not want to move away on their own or to their father's. Errol gave her a hundred dollars a week, something unusual for a ghetto man. Her children all pitched in and gave her forty or fifty dollars here and there.

She moved to Tower Street away from Allman Town, when in 1972 the rich people started running away from the violence of downtown Kingston to St. Andrew and Canada and America. She squatted on a piece of land and built with second-hand wood and zinc one bedroom in 1973; she added another room in 1975; then a kitchen was built in 1978; and finally a big bedroom in 1984.

Her higglering on Victoria Avenue became well known, and she brought in her aunt to help now and then. She brought home all the over-ripe produce that she sold on Victoria Avenue, adding a dumpling here and there, and filling the pot with an extra breadfruit from a neighbour or well-wisher. During Hurricane Gilbert, her food stall blew down, so she had to take a job. It was a great sorrow for her. She prayed to God night and day to provide for her and her children. They too were not allowed to waste time; they worked at their jobs and at her house. Thus, when we hired Claudette at Faith Centre, she was able to take on a double shift.

At work in our residence for the poor—young people physically and mentally handicapped as well as old people—Claudette simply felt that she had expanded her family: sixty people plus thirty school children plus workers to feed on a daily basis. Now Claudette does not want to go back to her higglering. Her children urged her to rebuild her food stall, but she simply said, "Me like the pickney them, and the whole heap of poor people." She is a mother to all, feeding them, cleaning them, comforting them. Claudette is a mother to her twelve children and to their children, and she is mother to other countless people who live at and pass through Faith Centre. She is a mother, a spiritual mother of Jamaica's poor, always willing to take in yet another homeless person, always ready to stretch the food and her arms wide open to all of suffering humanity.

Like so many women in Jamaica, she has no husband, but she is wedded to God and to the impossible ideal of loving all, no matter who, no matter how. Her strength could only be explained as a gift of grace from God in service of His kingdom here on earth.

Chapter Nine

....

"My son, do not despise the Lord's discipline
or be weary of his reproof,
for the Lord reproves him whom he loves."

Prov 3:12-12a

CLAUDETTE is not able to fight. She is a quiet woman today with sad eyes and brows high to the centre above that slant down to the corner of her eyes like a question mark. Because she is slender, she gives the appearance of height, and her hands and legs dangle like those of a puppet, which adds to the impression of being tall. She sat quietly at my desk looking out the window with a distant look.

"My son is dead. They called him Pusher, but his Christian name is Alphonso. The cocaine gang killed him. Yes, Father, he was involved with them.

"But, as a mother, I don't remember the beatings he gave me. Not even the time when him tear through my room as if some evil spirits take him and him rip up everything I own—my furniture, my clothes, even the little food I have—and threaten to break down the house unless I give him money.

"'Money, money, that's what I want. Money.'

"'What you want money for, Alphonso? Have your dinner, me son.'

"'I must have money. What kind of house is this? Not even five dollar dey bout?'

"Him flash him hand cross me face like a knife. And I fall back. Then him beat me and kick me, him own mother. It was the cocaine make him do it. That is not of his nature.

"It's a gang of them. Them do it. Is bad company make him do it. Them sit down all day long. Then young boy from uptown come down and buy it."

"You sure that is so, Claudette? A young boy from uptown?"

"Yes, Father. Sometime you see them. Not only him. There is a girl. She flash round in a car, and she bring bands of young people. Them have money. Then the ghetto youths sell it to them. I see them take it myself with me own eyes."

"They come to buy or sell?"

"Me no know. Maybe is to sell too. But me know for sure I see them take it as if is buy them buying cocaine."

"How come Alphonso get mixed up?"

"Pure frustration. Him business bruk down. The buying and selling never work. And him like sweet things. As I tell you, him used to buy expensive things give me. And the clothes him wear come straight from America.

"But Alphonso, him is a sweet, sweet person. The cocaine was not his true nature. He was quiet and kind as a youth. When I took sick with a slip disc, I couldn't move. Him used to do a little cooking and boil bush tea. The room he used to dust and even wash me clothes. And you know, Jamaican man don't wash woman things because them say it is wrong to touch clothes or food soiled with blood that woman give off. But all that him put out him mind. And him bring water and speak nicely to me. 'Mama, what you want?' And him would put him hand on me head and rub down me foot them because of the pain.

"One day the pain got too much and him take me in a taxi. And when I was in casualty at KPH. I was supposed to go to the

X-ray room. But there was no one to carry me and no stretcher. Alphonso lift me up like a baby in his arms. Imagine him is son to me and me is his mother and him lift me so strong and gentle. Not even him father would show me that love. When I remember that, I cry.

"At first I used to wonder, where Alphonso getting them things? Two years before the boys them shot him, Alphonso used to buy and sell little things-biscuits, suck-suck, chocolate. But then he used to bring things to me. Clothes and all kinds of expensive things. I used to feel glad, and I remember laughing when him bring me some pretty little earrings and things. But then sometime him never have anything. And him used to fidget and leave him dinner behind.

"Then him would get vex and fight and quarrel. One night him return home, him eyes red like fire. Him wake up all the pickney them and start beat them up. Is six pickney we have in that one room. So when him come home and start earning on, it was like cockroaches in a match box. We couldn't run anywhere and him is a strong twenty-two-year-old boy.

"Him leave and go to St. Ann's Bay down at Lime Hall. But when him come back, two weeks later, them shot him dead."

*   *   *

When Alphonso was a teenager, he had a compulsion to go back to the country. His daddy, Horace, had a beautiful piece of land at the foot of hills that stood like soldiers side by side guarding the community of people who dwelled at Lime Hall. Alphonso remembered how as a boy he and his four sisters and brothers sat in the grass in the open field of their father's farm land and watched the clouds walk across the sky. They would get lost in contemplating the clouds against the immense blue of the sky.

The clouds never stopped being a family. They travelled like a family, one flock of little lambs, with their mama and papa travelling in a definite direction as if guided by a shepherd.

Alphonso used to play with his imagination. "Look, there is one family now, one thick cloud. They must be at dinner now or at prayer." When the clouds divided but travelled in the same direction, he remarked, "Everyone going to school and work; mama at home, papa at planting yams. But everybody still together."

When the family broke Up, Alphonso s life was shattered. Horace used to sell the produce from his farm. But he got into company and didn't return home till next morning. He was out drinking, playing dominoes, and whoring. The children knew mama was vexed. Week after week stretched into years. Then he began beating her and the children mercilessly. "Where is the money," she would ask him. "How will the pickney go to school? You can't see how the children them clothes tear up and them have no shoes?"

The children stayed away from home more and more. They even stayed away from the field owned by their daddy. Instead they went down by the river, where the waters laughed rather than shed tears.

Alphonso was a true child of nature. He climbed the waterfalls, full of wonder at the creation and God's goodness. The river was abundant and so happy. "Why can't my father be so?"

The children swung on the vines that clung to the giant trees like hair from a human head. Everywhere was shady and secret, away from the turmoil and suffering. Joyfully they leapt in the air and fell in the pool of water beneath them. Then they would roll with the river, down, down the cascading waterfalls. Then finally out in the open under the warm open skies near the sea. The water was cool, and the sun was warm. This was heaven.

Then back to hell. One day Horace beat little Annie so hard with a tamarind stick that she bled. Then he chased down the bigger children. They had stripped down a mango tree and eaten and distributed the fruit among their friends.

Claudette took the children from the country to the yard where her mother had lived, in the slums of central Kingston. To her shame, all the rooms were occupied, and she had to beg to occupy the one where her mother had died.

Claudette warned the children not to keep bad company. But the children had known only a life of innocence and trust in everything and everyone. Two of the daughters had babies in their early teenage days. Alphonso was bitter. He loved his family, but he hated Kingston. Running between the country and the city, he dropped out of school. Alphonso got desperate. He tried buying and selling small goods to help himself and his family; it didn't work. Frustration led to ganja, and ganja smoking required ganja selling.

"When you start that bad habit, Alphonso?"

"Is natural, mama. Is part of the culture. No big deal."

Two years later, there was no work, and one more baby came. Alphonso took to stealing: robbing houses, robbing passersby on King Street, robbing even the other poor people in the ghetto. Then depression set in; he needed a high, higher than ganja could provide. Cocaine! He had to get a fix, from every now and then, to now, now, every moment, every day. That's when he beat up his mother and nearly tore the house down in search of money or objects to sell for money.

Then he broke down and cried, "Mama, no, me is not like me father. I don't want to beat you and lick the little ones them. But I can't make it, mama. I killing you and the pickney them."

"Go back to the country, Alphonso. That's where you belong."

"But daddy is not good."

"Talk to him. Maybe him will change. But get out of this rat hole."

Claudette said, "When Alphonso came back to visit me, him change. Him smile and him eyes clean like sky when him talk how the yam plant was like a youth, and the leaves start curl and wrap round the stick till it turn man.

"One day I told him, 'Go down to you auntie and pick up a money for me.' But him buck-up Khus-Khus on Matches Lane. One of the boys them spy him. 'Hey, is not Pusher that?' People say that Alphonso did hold a man name Percy long ago and tief off him ring. But that was Khus-Khus best cocaine customer who is a rich man son. Khus-Khus come up to Phonso and say, 'We could dust you off, you make me lose me uptown dollars. But if you join me, everything cool.' Phonso told him, 'Just rest it, you hear. I cool.' He looked at the gang. They forced a gun on his side. One of the youth was sucking cocaine like a chalice from a pipe; one was sniffing it; another smoked it mixed with ganja. Alphonso pretended to smoke it, but he was not inhaling. Khus-Khus said, 'I check you tonight.'

"But he gave up the cocaine, Father. For that I give thanks.

"At six o'clock that night, some neighbours call me. 'Come Claudette, come. The boys them shot Alphonso.'"

Claudette called out, 'Jesus Christ,' and stiffened suddenly like an animal struck by a bullet. Then she sprang up from her bed and left for KPH like a woman possessed.

In her long bony arms she enfolded the body of her dead son. The boy's feet still kicked. She kissed the lips of her boy still warm with life. Her long hair covered his face. Slowly the tears fell from her eyes. She was Mother Mary as she stripped off his shirt and wiped the blood from his body. She rocked him to and fro and murmured, "My baby."

Chapter Ten

....

"Blessed is he who considers the poor!
The Lord delivers him
in the day of trouble;
the Lord protects him
and keeps him alive;
he is called blessed in the land."

Ps 41:1-2

L EICESTER Lipton died. He will be buried tomorrow at Calvary Cemetery. What a man! Eighty-seven years and how he could tell tales that were the truth. He was the only white man at Jacob's Well. There aren't too many white men in Jamaica who are poor, and our homes are for the destitute.

Leicester sat down, legs crossed, and a cup of cocoa in his hand. "Good morning, Father. I'm grateful to be here."

"It is my pleasure to have you."

"You must wonder what a man like myself is doing here."

Leicester spoke with pride as he described the days when he wore a dark blue blazer, cap, and neck tie to school. Those were the glory days, and he played sunlight cricket and second eleven football as a school boy. Immediately after high school, he procured a job, and he never left it until the day he retired.

"I never married, Father. Too much trouble." He sniffed. "I like my independence."

When Brother Brian received the telephone call he was sceptical. The police reported, "An old man is living alone. He tried to hang himself." Brother Brian hurried to Red Hills, at the lookout, where Sterling Castle is. Although destitution and homelessness are our business, we could attend to a man who lived in a mansion and who had tried to kill himself.

The old gardener ran barefooted to meet Brother Brian. "Him was hanging from the ceiling. I cut him down wid me cutlass. A piece of cloth was round him neck." The gardener pointed excitedly to the wooden beam across the ceiling. "There he hang." The old white man lay curled up on the floor, weeping.

It was strange to see in this fine house pieces of dry sticks, a coal stove, ashes, dirty spoons and forks in the comer of the living room, the same as in the ghetto. But then the loss of self-respect and dignity perhaps symbolizes itself the same everywhere. Contrasted with this debris were the modern stone walls, fine bedrooms, elegant with curtains and mahogany furniture gone black with smoke and soot.

"I have nowhere to go. My sister from Scotland visited me this morning. She told me to get out, the new owners wanted me out. I didn't know what to do so I tried to hang myself."

Brother Brian was surprised to find out that Ins sister had actually picked up a chair and told him to stand on it. She had slung a piece of torn cloth around the beam and invited him to place his neck in the noose. Then she had left. At eighty-six he was an old man, and she preferred to see him dead.

"The mansion had been sold. Nobody told me. The gardener was kind enough to let me in at night. The new owner didn't want to lock me out himself. Sometimes I just roamed the streets at nights and lay down where I could. Sometimes I came to the mansion."

At Jacobs Well, he was grateful and at home. It gave a new chapter to his life. "Father, give me a blessing." I would hold his head and pray for his health and God's blessings. Then he would continue his life story.

I am from a family of six. Even body left for Scotland where my parents came from. But I loved the cricket and dominoes. You see, Father, I was a child too much, trusting everyone, including my boss. I loved my job. I used to be head of stores for years, masterminding what came in, what went out. I used to count the goods and designate this to this place and that to that place. And the boys obeyed me. Then I became an executive.

"When old age took me, I couldn't live alone any longer. My relatives took me at Sterling Castle. I loved the company. All my drinking companions had gone and got married. One day my sister Marcia told me, 'Leicester, you got your compensation and your own house on Belmont Road. You ought to be grateful for all we have done for you.' I felt ashamed and told her she could have everything I owned. I sold my little house and gave her the thirty-thousand dollars I had in the bank. She told me I could continue to live in the mansion. That was the last time I saw her until recently.

"But I don t blame her. When her children grew up, they went to parties every night. They used to get drunk and what have you. My sister's husband David didn't stay in the house. He had a woman or women. Marcia used to mumble to herself, 'Why am I staying in this place? Jamaica has nothing more to offer me.' For six years, I lived in the mansion alone.

"Father, you see all those people," meaning the residents at Jacob's Well, the retarded, the old people, the blind, and the lame. "They are more loving than my family." Marguerite encouraged him to sweep as he told his story. "And this," he turned to Marguerite, "is my true sister." He swept the floor and under the beds. You could hear his bones creak like footsteps in an old haunted house. He loved to talk, and the sweeping was more an interruption to his primary occupation. "Look at everybody helping one another." Old Kenneth was repairing

the clothes lines. Lloyd was picking up the chimmeys and dis-
posing the urine from the night before. Gloria and Sugar, two
old ladies, were in the kitchen peeling yams. Ralph was in the
yard sweeping. Hyacinth and the wheelchair residents were
telling tales and jokes under the ackee tree.

"Yes, I am ready to die."

Marguerite said, "No, Mr. Lipton, you mustn't say that."

"But it is the truth. I am ready."

Emphysema and arthritis were getting the better of him. He
would often lie tired in bed, breathing hard. Sometimes his
spirit would get low. One day Marguerite heard him cry out,
"God, God, I love you. You hear me? The poor children and
old people: I didn't help them." Marguerite held his hands
and prayed with him. He looked at her and smiled. "I thought I
was in heaven. My father is calling me home. I don't mind.
I'm old."

That day you could see the bones more than you could see
his face and body. The rib cage was like a skeleton on that bed.
You could also see the bones in his legs hinged to his hip bones.
His face was also all bone—the deep-set eyes, though blue, were
dark, sunken into his forehead, and his hooked nose protruded
like a hawk. Yet he was not morbid, but beautiful. A smile never
left his face, and a light shone from the sunken eyes. In truth,
there was no more flesh left on that body, only spirit, a lumi-
nous and effusive spirit. All his body had been ripped away, and
there was only the soul of Mister Lipton laid bare on the bed.

"I'm going to die today at eleven o'clock." He held on to
Marguerite. "Tell my friends."

Brother Murray, Marguerite, and the residents were by his
bedside. He told tales. Most didn't understand what he said,
but they liked hearing his voice. At eleven-fifteen in the morning, he was fully conscious. "I am passing away. The Lord is

waiting for me. I have told Him everything." He closed his eyes and smiled. Then he mumbled the Rosary with every-one. They finished the first three Glorious Mysteries. Then he opened his eyes for the last time and lifted his right hand towards Marguerite. "Good-bye." She took his hand; then he slipped away. The group around the deathbed began the fourth Glorious Mystery, the Assumption: "Our Father in heaven. . . ."

Brothers in Christ with their Daddy.

Chapter Eleven

·····························

"Naked I came from my mother's womb,
naked I shall return.
Yahweh gave, Yahweh has taken away.
Blessed be the name of the Lord."

Job 1:21

HAPPINESS. It eludes most of us. There is a great confu-sion between pleasure of the senses and the happiness that can only come about by simple living and service of our fellow men. At the centre of happiness is God, He loving us and we loving Him. It gives us a life lived in absolute joy and self-fulfilment. We are meant for God. Happiness is predefined: it is obtained only in Him who is God, our experience with the Almighty, our Maker, our beloved Father in Heaven. We can-not set up our own goals for happiness. The soul of man cannot be satisfied except in union with God: our oneness of heart and mind with Him. The fulfilment of His will is our work. Only then is there stillness of the soul. As plants are meant for light, man is meant for God.

A pure heart is cleansed of any desire other than the love of the heavenly Father. Nothing else is of importance or of value in life—no wealth, no goods, no worldly ambition, no politics, no intellectual knowledge, no power. In fact, it is the poor one of Yahweh who reaches God: the humble man, broken, defeated, stripped of everything as happened to Job who became totally the child of God. When we are humbled, stripped of everything, we are like an empty room, ready to

receive everything God is. Free of any baggage, we can journey lightly and in freedom to God. Then He pours out His
life and His blessings on us. We would have given up everything, all natural desires, by the power of His supernatural
grace. Having nothing and being nothing, we are clean, pure
of heart, and He descends into our lives and lifts us to the
greatest heights of ecstasy and happiness. What Carlo Caretto
says is correct: "Nothing can give men greater consolation
than the cry that springs from his mouth when he is caught
up in the struggle with no defence but his own weakness, who
nevertheless with unshakable confidence in God, holds on to
him." When God hears our cry, He comes to us and gives us
His presence.

Humility: that is the greatest of the Christian virtues. It leads
us to God. Pride is the ugliest and most common of our vices.
It makes us self-centred and separated from God; but when we
realize our total dependence on God, then we bend to His will
and listen to His voice. We are not too busy obtaining our own
goals, but we are watching, listening for that one person, He
who is our happiness and total self-fulfilment.

Sometimes it is in freedom that we give up everything in
our search for happiness; sometimes it is by force that God
takes away everything, strips us naked so that we are forced to
call upon His name. Whichever, it is a terrifying experience.
It means groping in the dark, having nothing but this hungry
desire for life, for meaning, for happiness. We yell, "God, why
have you forsaken me." The most genuine of prayers is hurled
from the depths of our being. It is deep calling upon deep, the
prelude to a life of the soul filled with God's grace rather than
the shallow pleasures of this world. This cry is the desperation
of the soul calling out in the dark night.

Hear my prayer, O Lord; give ear to my supplications!
I remember the days of old,
    I meditate on all that thou hast done;
    I muse on what thy hands have wrought.
I stretch out my hands to thee;
    my soul thirsts for thee like parched land.
    Make haste to answer me, O Lord!
    My spirit fails!
Hide not thy face from me,
    lest I be like those who go down to the Pit.
Let me hear in the morning of thy steadfast love,
    for in thee I put my trust.
Teach me the way I should go,
    for to thee I lift up my soul.

                                    Ps 143:1a, 5-8

We are the children of Papa St. John Paul II. He visits Missionaries of
the Poor with Archbishop Samuel Carter. August 1993.

Chapter Twelve

....

"Sarah said, 'God has made laughter for me.'"

Gen 21:6a

A S I arrived at Faith Centre New Year's Day, Mr. Spencer told me that henceforth I would have to address Mr. Martin as Your Majesty.

"What is this?"

"Yes, it's true. We had a crowning last night."

Faith Centre. The male dormitory. New Year's Eve, there was a crowning. All the men were gathered round telling jokes late into the night waiting for the new year to blow in. There was much cackling as each one recounted funny incidents from the past. How Desmond lost control in the night and urinated in his bed and the urine fell from the top bunk to the bottom, and Mr. Palmer had a dream that it rained. How Frankie fell in love with an old woman Helen, a volunteer, and when he ran over to welcome her, his pants fell off. On and on. Then Mr. Martin blew his mouth organ, and the feeble old men and Down's syndrome men danced the old Jamaican mento. Those who are crippled clapped hands and hooted. Hips shook, feet stamped, and voices howled off tune.

Suddenly Mr. Spencer announced, "The New Year is coining in. We need a new king of the dormitory to rule over this kingdom so there is justice and fairness and human rights observed." There was much commotion and excitement. Three men were nominated: Carl, because he works so hard and is so generous; Mr. Matthews, because of his strictness and because he is very wise; and Mr. Martin, because he is so wealthy, having twenty-five dollars in his savings. But Carl can't speak, so there would be no royal speeches. Mr. Matthews is in a wheelchair and so couldn't lead the residents into battle. So Mr. Martin was crowned the king of Faith Centre and the universe. A chimmey was put on top of his head. It fitted perfectly. An old mop was placed in his right hand and a red blanket thrown over his shoulders. There was much clapping and much laughter. Then the throne speech.

"Ladies and gentlemen, I don't know why the girls like me so. But I am a shy man. Many have told me I am a handsome man, but I don't really believe it. Many say I am very wise, but they are exaggerating. I have a little knowledge, but I don't believe I have full knowledge, not yet anyway. But I do know I am a just man, a good man, a man who gets along with people.

"I am also the humblest man in the world, and I never boast. For this I believe I was made a king. There are dangers, however. I hope to get married soon. A few girls around town like me. But I don't find the right girl yet. A man of my ability don't want nobody to marry me because of my money. The thief them in this dormitory take away ten dollars of my Christmas money. Also some of you crown me because I have twenty-five dollars more. And, you know, my mother and sister are in America, and Miss Weatherby, my sister, lives in Harbour View. I am a man of great ability, but I don't want you the people to live off me. But still, I accept my responsibility as king."

Nathan, Charles, Johnson, Spencer, and all the Down's syndrome and retarded men cheered. Then the king, Mr. Martin, pulled out his harmonica and played. The New Year was rung in.

They shared crackers and cocoa and sang Auld Lang Syne. Then they turned off the lights. The women in the dormitory next door shouted that they must shut up. They wanted to go to sleep.

"Yes, Father, it was quite a night. You know, if we don't laugh, Jesus not with us in our heart."

I too have a home with the Brothers.

Chapter Thirteen

"Then children were brought to him that he might lay his hands on them and pray. The disciples rebuked the people; but Jesus said, 'Let the children come, to me, and do not hinder them; for to such belongs the kingdom of heaven.'"

Mt 19:13-14

"GOD cursed Violet and sent her a child with the brain of a fool. She used to be bad and run like a Lego beast on the street, so when the baby was born, God punished her. She hide the boy child in her back room and lock him up. Frankie used to sit down as if in a prison, and when people wasn't around, him used to sweep the house and the backyard. But Violet used to take set on him; she hated him like sin. Poor Frankie couldn't do any harm. Him would just smile and say, 'Mama, don't hit me.'

"Is me sister pickney. She gone to England and married. But Frankie is a retarded man now. Me can't take care of him no more. Me is a poor woman with me own worries to contend with."

Alice left Frankie with us. He is a big baby whale who flops around and gives everybody a hug. He and the other Down's syndrome men are our welcoming committee at Faith Centre. Everybody who comes to visit us will be greeted by a great big smile, a handshake, and a hug, all dealt out with absolute trust and a confidence that love is the most obvious of activities. Frankie is the fattest of them; his belly hangs far in front of his pants which droop precariously on the edge of his protruding bottom. His jet black face is a half-moon smile, all dimples, and he has two white buttons for eyes.

"Fadda! Me bredda come."

In walked a tall slender rastaman. The hair was all dreadlocks, long and wrapped in torches, in celebration of his defiance against society. Frankie's arms were wrapped around him, and he responded warmly.

"Glad to meet you, sir."

"Happy to meet you. Sit down."

"Is all right, sir, I just came to check out Frankie."

"You must come and visit him often."

"If God spare."

"You want to take him home?"

"Is Concrete Jungle where I live. And me can barely survive."

"All right, man, but come visit him."

They spent the day together. The rastaman really loves his brother Frankie. They had arms around each other all day long. When the day was done, he held Frankie's hand and wished him good-bye. Frankie enveloped his brother with a hug and mushy kiss. All the defiance of the rastaman melted away.

Frankie was so happy. He went around telling everybody, "Me bredda come. Me bredda come." Old Harrison, a cripple who lives in our residence, was swept out of his bed. Frankie lifted him up at bath time and wheeled him around in circles and scared the living daylights out of Harrison. But everybody laughed. Harrison is a sophisticated old man who barks orders from his wheelchair and speaks of his past as though he were some descendant from royalty.

"Put me down. I say put me down, Frankie."

Bur Frankie was so happy, he kept wheeling Harrison around. Then he would pretend to be putting Harrison in the big washtub but lifted him high again. Everybody laughed. Suddenly Frankie dumped Harrison in the washtub and soaped him down. Our playful baby whale began splashing Harrison with water all over his face. Harrison began seriously to lose his cool. But Frankie stroked his face, smiled his half-moon smile, and said, "Me bredda come."

Frankie lifted Harrison and brought him to his bed, dried him, covered him, and brought him a glass of water. Harrison began telling bedtime stories. The other men gathered around and told their tales. There were jokes. The Down's syndrome men stood around the bed, all of Frankie's pals. And they laughed when everybody laughed and mimicked the gesticulations of every tale told by our residents. Frankie was just so overjoyed because "Me bredda come." And that spirit of love filled the residents for days.

Frankie and the Down's syndrome residents are by definition, love. But they are not fool-fool or stupid. They have an instinctive sense of right and wrong. They also possess a deep sense of fairness and justice. These beautiful Down's syndrome people are very special children: God's children. They live on love, and they live to love. They are basic elemental human nature, in all its beauty and simplicity. We know that if anyone has a Down's syndrome child, they can be sure that joy, laughter, and love have been given to them as a special gift from God. We welcome these gifts with delight.

*   *   *

Garth is like a big water baby, full of cuddles and a dimpled smile. When he laughs, he lets out a big bellow; when he talks, he grunts. After lunch, he curls up like a baby in a chair, his mouth open and drooling, basking in the afternoon sun.

Garth loves to wash clothes. It doesn't matter how dirty they are. And he empties the dummies with such an air of uncon- cern and dignity. He shows off the chimmey, holding it aloft, then pours the urine in the toilet like a waiter pouring wine. If he knows you are watching him, he laughs and laughs.

I love Garth. The Brothers love Garth. Who doesn't love Garth? Strange mystery, this God of ours, to have made people like Garth—a little child in a man's body. A big lovable, hug- gable baby. Sometimes in our idle dreams, we wish that a little infant so pretty would remain innocent forever. Well, here it is embodied in Garth and all our Down's syndrome adults.

Garth is the essence of love, and he lives in trust. People are good: he believes that, and all he wants is to hug and be hugged. Yes, he will work. He will tidy and clean the rooms. But is work the primary intention of God for a Down's syndrome person? Or is it a value superimposed by our productive-mad world? I don't see why Garth should produce. Love—sweet and innocent and pure—he produces, not an excess commodity in our modem world. Nor do I see any great value in upgrading Garth's intellectual skills. God did not bless him with a mind to think deeply or read, but he doesn't feel inferior. His heart is what he has.

That most beautiful and marvellous of human virtues is abundant in Garth. God is love, and he makes this world so full of surprises, with so many different people, each according to His will. St. Paul talks about love: it is the greatest of the virtues, and it has the power to transform our world. We are trans- formed by the Down's syndrome people in our residences. We love and are loved by Harold, Frankie, Wayne, and Garth. They are a tribute to God Himself. They bring the love of God to us, and we see God's wonderful sense of humour and love in them.

Garth doesn't require much, not money, not many changes of clothes. Yes, he loves food, but he will eat anything he is given and with much relish and a smile. There are many worries in the world because our modern world requires that we have so much. We sophisticated people battle and compete to acquire so much, intellectually and financially. We must have the best for ourselves and our children. There are so many goods that are there to be had: so we miss the flowers, the trees, the birds of the air, and each other.

There is no ambition, no battle for power, no pomp, no falsehood, no hypocrisy in the Down's syndrome people. There may be a little pensiveness, a little laziness; a sexual interest appears as part of the Down's syndrome's humanity. But there is childhood, humility, and simplicity in them. There is no deviousness as they fold us in their arms.

I like going to the beach with Garth. I find in him the way to regain innocence. With him, I can delight in Brother Sun, Sister Moon, the pelicans and the clouds sailing in the clear blue sky. And I can float on the ocean of faith, buoyed up by God's grace and His fatherly love.

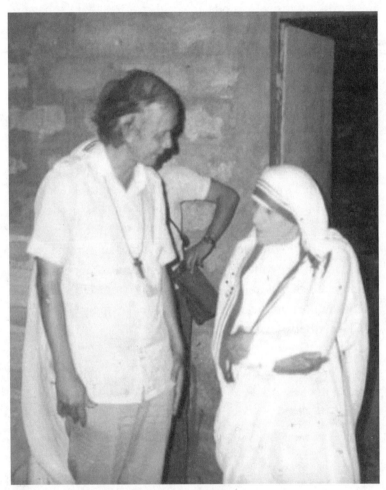

Mother Teresa at Faith Centre. July 9, 1986.

Chapter Fourteen

*"Then the King will say to those at his right hand,
'Come, O blessed of my Father, inherit the kingdom
prepared for you from the foundation of the world;
for I was hungry and you gave, me food, I was thirsty
and you gave me drink, I was a stranger and you wel-
comed me, I was naked and you clothed me, I was sick
and you visited me, I was in prison and you came to
me.' Then the righteous will answer him, 'Lord, when
did we see thee hungry and feed thee, or thirsty and
give thee drink? And when did we see thee a stranger
and welcome thee, wor naked and clothe thee? And
when did we see thee sick or in prison and visit thee?'
And the King will answer them, 'Truly I say to you,
as you did it to one of the least of these my brethren,
you did it to me.'"*

Mt 25:34-40

MOTHER Teresa visited Faith Centre! That was an honour—one person the world acknowledges to be a saint. It was an unexpected joy! She is pure spirit, a little bird of a woman, her face deeply lined, but alert with life and intelligence. Transcending age and individual motherhood, she is the mother of three thousand nuns and countless poor people in seventy-five countries. She is joy, and she brought joy to our homeless residents. She laughed, prayed, blessed our residents and murmured, "Beautiful," as she personally greeted each one of our homeless. Worn sandals on her feet, she walked humbly

59

among them and extended her hand again and again to clasp warmly the hand of each person.

Mr. Harrison in his wheelchair sang for her "I Got a Girl." Blind Mr. Martin played "Beautiful Dreamer" on his harmonica. Her face was filled with light and pleasure. She played with our retarded children and young adults. Taking the hand of Harold, one of our Down's syndrome men, she counted off on his fingers, "Do - it - un - to - me." He laughed and imitated her action.

She spoke to the women and men from the ghetto who gathered in our yard. "Love one another. Find Christ in one another." She knew there was great suffering among the poor but told them, "Pain is Christ's; don't waste it! Christ wants you to carry the Cross. Take it and be one with him."

She invited our Brothers to visit with her. We went barefooted to the chapel. She reminded us, "Silence brings prayer, prayer brings God, God leads us to service, and service brings us peace." Then she stated repeatedly, "We are not social workers. Social workers work for money. We work for a person, Christ." At the end, she asked us to pray for her.

When we met the next morning, I told her she must write to the Prime Minister and ask for the building on Tower Street where her sisters might care for homeless poor. She scribbled the letter of request on the page of a school exercise book. The Prime Minister gave her the building for fifty years' use.

She advised us to do small things, but with great love. This sums up what I want at the Faith Centre which has brought hope and joy to so many, but most of all to the Brothers. Do small things with great love: to be in the middle of the slums, to be feeding the hungry, to be caring for the sick, to be clothing the naked, to be visiting the prisoner. This is to be at the very heart of life and death. Thank God for the poor, God's gift to us!

Chapter Fifteen

"Who shall separate us from the love of Christ?
Shall tribulation, or distress, or persecution, or fam-
ine, or nakedness, or peril, or sword?"

Rom 8:35

A T the police station, the officer brought Bedford to me. Bedford looked defeated and barely smiled when he sat down in the visitor's area of the police station.

"Were the police rough with you?" I saw swellings on his hands.

"Police nearly bruk me bones."

"What are the charges?"

"I told Fern Gully the police would come and kill the two of we. I told him to float; don't stay at my place. But him have no place to lay him head. Fern Gully come round the other day, but I know they would catch him cause of the fact that if you rob tourist you nah get off."

"You shouldn't harbour a man who committed theft, Bedford."

"Is me cousin. Father. Him is me idren."

I asked him why the police hit him.

"I did run, Father. I told them that is a friend sleeping in the back room. They asked me, 'Where Fern Gully dey?' 'Him down the street, boss. Is there him sleep.' When they were looking in my back room, Fern Gully jumped up, gun was by his head.

"'Who you is, boy?' Fern Gully gave a false name. They came and asked me. 'Is me cousin from the country.' Fern Gully

61

changed his mind and told the truth. 'If they gwine kill me, let them kill me.' They pulled him out of bed. 'Bedford, you lie to me, boy?' I try protect me face, that is how I get lick on me hand."

"Bedford, what can I bring you?"

"Me baby-mother gwine get bail for me. I want to get out fast. Me can't stand dis ya jail."

"You must pray, Bedford."

"Yes, Father." I sat with him for a while in silence. Tears came to his eyes. Bedford, poor Bedford, a good man without a chance. He was trapped in a snake pit in the ghetto. He had broken up fights in the ghetto among the youths. He had been through a conversion, turning away from gambling and stealing to God. Now his spirit was broken. Even in trying to help his cousin Fern Gully, he was caught for harbouring a criminal.

Instead of turning to ganja as Fern Gully did in prison, Bedford turned to God. He talked about the Promised Land and a new generation of youths. God would give the children and the women new hearts. They would want nothing else but to love one another. The police and JDF would become fathers of the poor, and the rich would join hands with the poor. All the poor people needed was a little food, a little job, and lots of respect for one another. All night long, all day long, he prayed. While he was in prison, Bedford saw himself like John the Baptist in the desert. After prison, he would become a preacher.

I had watched Bedford mature. He was baptized, confirmed, went to confession, and came to Mass and communion every Sunday. He never took the rosary from around his neck. And he always had a little pocketbook Bible he carried around with him in his shirt pocket.

We sat and prayed for a while. "Tell me little youth dem I soon come, you hear, Father?" Bedford has two little children, a boy and a girl. "Someday I will get out. I will not be defeated. I will conquer with my God." I told him, "We will give them a little food everyday. The Brothers will take care of them."

"Tell me baby-mother I send me love."

"I will tell her."

"Don't worry bout me, you hear, Father. God is with me."

"How is Fern Gully," asked Bedford. "I feel sorry for him, you see. Father. Things bad for me, but it badder fe Fern Gully. At least me have me God. Last night I dream of angels and when I wake up I feel God inside of me, powerful and wonderful inside me chest. I praise Him and give Him thanks and say, 'How wonderful you are.' And I still feel Him in me chest. Tell Fern Gully about this God, Father. A fe we God him live inside a we, we prisoners. Tell Fern Gully and tell Him our God is love."

Our men have lost their way; bring them back, Lord.

Chapter Sixteen

....

"Hear, O women, the word of the Lord,
and let your ear receive the word of his mouth;
teach to your daughters a lament,
and each to her neighbour a dirge.
For death has come up into our windows,
it has entered our palaces,
cutting off the children from the streets
and the young men from the squares."

Jer 9:20-21

THEY call him Fern Gully. That's where he comes from. It got too hot in Ocho Rios where he and two boys were chased by the police for selling spliffs and harassing tourists. The people on the sidewalk were vexed and told the police his name. One night the police raided his shack and found a gun. The police tried to bag him, but Fern Gully flew away like a night owl. Myth has it that he was hit six times; his corpse should have fallen to the ground, but he flew away in the form of a bird.

Fem Gully fled to Kingston, in the ghetto. His cousin Bedford had lived as a boy with him in Ocho Rios, but Bedford moved to the city after his mother died and his father took off for New York. Fern Gully now moved in with Bedford in Kingston. Bedford set up Fern Gully with a suck-suck and biscuit business, right outside of St. Aloysius primary. But the competition was stiff and the kids didn't have the money. Fern Gully went back to Bedford and told him, "Things thin. I need to show people more types of goods." Bedford helped him with some additional money. Fern Gully set up a shop and expanded into jerk chicken, festival, bulla cake, and box juice. Things did not improve. Bedford told him he had to pay him back.

Fern Gully knew Bedford was serious. He saw a foreigner walking along East Queen Street. It was said the man was attending the conference at the Seabed Conference Centre. Fern Gully used a knife and drew the foreigner down the side of a bridge and then down by the gully. He robbed him of three hundred American dollars. An old lady passing by yelled, "Thief," but Fern Gully threw away the briefcase and flew down the gully heading towards Harbour Street.

When he got to the street, he pulled the towel from his back pocket and wrapped it around his neck and hitched his dark glasses to cover his eyes. Then he hurried along the street and contemplated, "I want to disappear, get out of this country. I want to go to foreign and make some serious breads." He meant the foreigner no harm, but the opportunity was there. "So it go." Fern Gully felt bad that he hadn't paid back Bedford who had been so kind to him. The foreigner was just there, and white foreigners always have money. He took the money out of his pocket. "This is easy breads. Look how I worked nine months and don't see this kind of money." Still, he didn't want to be a thief. "I want to go to foreign; there I can earn an honest breads. I must go to New York or Miami. Money dey bout. Yes, man."

The police got a report from the foreigner and were after Fern Gully. Bedford told him, "Don't come back." Fern Gully had nowhere to go. He slept here and there. One night he slept on the side of the street outside First Baptist Church on East Queen Street. "Lord, what is this? Where is me life going? Mama did warn me to go to school. Papa lash me and tell me, me worthless. I accept it. When I check it, if you born poor and illiterate, is down the road you going to slide. I accept that I had to run to Kingston. Maybe God intend for me to be a thief. For him didn't intend for me to go hungry. God want me fe eat food, for me is fe Him own pickney. Lord, what to do?"

When things cooled down, Fern Gully went back to Bedford. Bedford told him, "You can't stay here." Fern Gully told him, "God don't want me to sleep on the street." Bedford told him okay. "Stay, but stay cool." Fern Gully abandoned the shop. There was a sadness in him, like a wailing inside. Another failure. He sang to himself, "If I had the wings of a dove, I would fly, fly away, fly away, fly away, and be at rest."

Bedford told him, "Go to Faith Centre and see one of the Brothers." Fern Gully didn't want to go, but Bedford reasoned with him. "Maybe they can get you a job."

"But I not in anything with the Brothers."

"Go." That's when Fern Gully came and told the whole story. At the last moment, he changed his mind, he didn't ask for a job.

"Can't you get me a visa, Father? I want to fly away to America."

"You are asking for worries. Fern Gully. America is a hard life. It requires an education. Otherwise you get into drugs and before you know, you are part of a posse."

Fern Gully smiled. "If God intend me to be a part of a posse, a so it go. I accept anything. But don't you agree, God don't want me to starve?"

"Work, Fern Gully."

"And if there is no work."

I was silent. "There must be work."

"Where, Father?"

"I will see. But you are a thief, Fern Gully." It was his time to be silent. "Let us pray." We prayed together. "Come back and see me tomorrow, Fern Gully." "Yes, Father."

That night a woman who works at the craft market detected Fern Gully at Bedford's gate. She sent her little girl to the police. The plain-clothes police walked on foot late that night. They kicked in the gate. This time Fern Gully couldn't fly. He sat up, closed his eyes, and quickly prayed, "I accept, God, whatever happen to me." The gun was pointed at his head.

Chapter Seventeen

"Thus the Lord God showed me: behold
a basket of summer fruit.
And he said, 'Amos, what do you see?'
And I said, 'A basket of summer fruit.'
Then the Lord said to me,
'The end has come upon my
people Israel;
I will never again pass by them.
The songs of the temple shall become
wailings in that day,'
says the Lord God;
'The dead bodies shall be many;
in every place they shall be cast
out in silence.'"

Amos 8:1-3

FERN Gully was raised in a family of five children. His mother was a thin woman with a shy smile. Even when the children had grown, she remained girlish and quiet. She still played like a girl with her children and had them braid her hair and put in plastic butterflies to hold it. Emma worshipped at the Church of Christ and brought up the kids to revere God and to stay by themselves. At night time, after a long day serving as a maid at Mrs. Wharton's, Emma would come home and make sure that the children's uniforms were clean for the next day. The two boys wouldn't stay around, and she always had to quarrel with John-John, later to be nicknamed Fern Gully, and

Stephen. They spent much of the evening with their sling shots or climbing the neighbour's trees for fruits.

While their brothers played, the little girls would help tidy the two rooms, wash and iron the clothes, and help their mother peel the vegetables. Mother Emma would boil yam and coco, and if there was meat, season and cook it down. Their father Ralph ran an old taxi cab, but hardly brought home any money because the cab was always breaking down, and he had two other baby-mothers who were at him night and day for a few dollars to take care of the pickney. No one doubted, moreover, that Ralph had other women aside from these, and spent the money on himself. The children saw him outside the gas station with box lunch and Red Stripe beer all the time. No wonder he didn't eat dinner when he came home. Emma wouldn't say much to him, however, for she didn't believe in losing her temper. Asthma attacked her: the consolation was that Emma died with her children and church sisters by her side. Before she died, Emma tried to pass the young ones off to friends, but they too were poor and couldn't attend to their own needs. After she passed away, the children got confused and ran wild. As for their father, he bought a bogus visa and left for America.

Fern Gully got that name because he set up a little tourist shop in Fern Gully, Ocho Rios, selling beads and bangles, belts and shirts. But being in the tourist business, he got into the quick cash-crop business, the quickest being ganja. When Reggae Sunsplash came to Montego Bay, he left his tourist shop of bric-a-bracs and jumped on a mini-van and made very quick cash, a few thousand dollars, just selling marijuana. But Reggae Sunsplash does not take place everyday, and he had to return to Fern Gully and try a thing again. The few dollars he made at his bamboo shop didn't make sense. So he got seriously into the ganja business.

When he returned to Ocho Rios, he felt a sudden panic that his life was wasting away. His only relief was to walk in the hills alone among the lush plants. He liked to be solitary in the woods. It made him feel like life was sweet again, simple again. In the countryside he was like a child again, back in his mother's womb, enclosed by the huge mysterious cave of trees and ferns. The long winding path which is Fern Gully was dark and cool. He would walk under the arch of trees. Then he would suddenly come to the open skies under the stars: diamonds of fireflies dancing above. It made him happy, and he would often sing the old songs he learned in church, and he would feel washed, purified by the renewing spirit of God in nature.

In St. Ann, he was never hungry, Fern Gully told me. "No matter where you go, Father, there is food. You learnt nature is a mother that feeds you. And when you want to bathe, you just jump ina di sea. Nothing fresher."

"Then why didn't you just settle down and be simple like your mother?"

"No increase in that, Father. When I see the money dey bout, it set up a different vibes: I can move forward with money. I can get piece of the action."

"How will you get money, Fern Gully?"

"It is there if you want to think of advancement." In his mind, advancement is just as easy as picking mangoes.

Fern Gully's psyche is still that of a simple, romantic primitive. Even money is a free thing like a fruit, to be given or easily earned and spent. Life to him is a matter of hunting, picking fruits, shooting birds, and a quick dip in the ocean. Nature is good, the world is good: the air he breathes and the food he eats are provided easily by the sky and the earth. Money is the same, or so he thinks, and he is angry when it doesn't come as easily. For him, life is free and easy and benevolent. What's there is there to be used: bounteous Mother Nature provided by the hand of God.

But in the meanwhile, Jamaica has changed. The land has been bought up. There are massive high-rise buildings and sleek hotels, cars are our feet, and dance-hall music has replaced the religious chants. Fern Gully is a simple country boy hyped up with a desire to be like that modern world about him. The truth is Fern Gully can't be because he is not properly equipped, as is the case of most of our poor simple and undereducated people in Jamaica. To create the false impression that life is still easy and beautiful as the sky above, our youth get revved up with ganja and cocaine, or they kill to obtain the cash and put on the paraphernalia of sophisticated youth such as they see on television, hip and energetic, living in the fast lane.

To Fern Gully, the goods of the modern American city are the stars and the moon. Fern Gully is angry because he cannot get them. Why can't he get them? As a nature person, he knows Mother Nature, fertile and always good to her promises. But the modern world has hung out the urban goods and laughed. "See it; you can't have it." The poor see the best money can buy in St. Ann, in St. Andrew, in Montego Bay, and I dare say everywhere in Jamaica. But they can't have it. "Cry your heart out. You can't have it." So far the city shops have not had their showcase windows splintered, but for how long? Fern Gully tells me, "I want my share now."

He has been given two years in prison. How dreadfully different this is from the beautiful mountains and hills, seas and rivers of Ocho Rios: cooped up in a cell with three other men, in a dark hole. He is in that cell sixteen hours a day, with only the harsh reality of prison and his escape dreams of a promised land of milk and honey.

I went to General Penitentiary and told Fern Gully about Bedford. He listened and closed his eyes and gave thanks for my tale about Bedford. Then he began to sing, "Amazing grace, how sweet the sound that saved a wretch like me."

Graffiti in the ghettos celebrating the life of God and His people.

Chapter Eighteen

....

"The Lord is gracious and merciful,
slow to anger and abounding in steadfast love.
The Lord is good to all,
and his compassion is over all that he has made."

Ps 145:8-9

THE Brothers were at Gun Court Christmas Eve. Two women were with us, Sister Ann Marie, a nurse who has given us volunteer medical service for many years, and Clarissa, a volunteer who originally came from Guyana but now lives in Toronto. It was funny to see demure Sister Ann Marie, in her veil and habit, surrounded and draped in the arms of some five big tough prisoners, and Clarissa, a proper lady with slightly graying hair and dainty glasses, completely surrounded by a hundred or more prisoners, mostly from the ghettoes.

The women laughed. The prisoners laughed. The women sang. The prisoners sang. Food was dished out, and the prisoners gave thanks. We prayed, preached, laughed, fed, and celebrated the birthday of the Prince of Peace—God with us, Emmanuel, the Son of God, the saviour of the world, the comforter of men.

I was astounded at the gentleness and mirth. I wanted so much to bring Christ to the prisoners. If only they knew the love of God! If only they could understand the joy of living in God!

"Struggle! Battle through life! Work, work until sweat becomes blood. But do not steal, do not take drugs, do not take

75

up guns. Be ready to struggle with your poverty, and hold your head high with dignity. Jesus is here. He is with us. He is born into your lives. He offers love. He takes up the Cross with you. Walk with him and never turn back on the road to Calvary, on the road to victory."

I believe that in the ghetto, in this society, as cruel as it is, if a man is decent and hard working, though he may never obtain the wages due to him, he will make it in life. We ourselves have sought labourers in our building and maintenance work. Others have asked us for workers too. By and large, every man who has asked for a job and then neither steals nor lies nor perpetrates violence has made out in life. I know ex-prisoners who are fanners, reporters, labourers, messengers, and guards who have forged ahead with life. Other ghetto men and women have put their hands to hard labour, menial work, and they are managing to squeeze out a living. But those who are hooked on fast living, fast wealth, and trickery are now hooked on drugs, guns, and theft. They do not hold jobs and are unemployable without serious rehabilitation.

There are jobs, not enough to be sure. But people are always looking for good workers. They are underpaid, but so is most everyone else in the nation. There is only one way. We must keep the law of God, and the law of love, and even though we are not given our just wage, we must struggle on.

"Why are you in jail?"

"I killed a man," said the prisoner.

I looked at his face. I saw there no hardness, no cruelty there. He explained, "A friend took my car. I went with him. He had a gun, and he gave me a gun. We both shot this friend of his."

He is rightly in jail. But he is filled with sorrow and truth and a desire for forgiveness.

"I broke into a house," said another.

"Drug trafficking."

"Robbery with aggravation."

This same group of men hugged the Catholic sister, embraced our female volunteer, begged for special blessings and sang their hearts out at the birthday of Jesus.

I couldn't believe it! We had food for exactly three hundred and sixty men. Everyone was fed. There was no line. I couldn't believe there was no wrangling for food, no quarrels over smaller portions. Some came and said, "I had mine already. Can I have a little more?" The superintendent was astounded also. He thought we had a system to make sure no one would be allowed to exploit the situation, but we didn't. In the rush we couldn't shut them all down in their cells and then distribute to perfection only so many plates for so many men.

God is in the hearts of the prisoners. They too want Christ. How foolish of me even to suspect otherwise.

They promised to pray for the Brothers and all our kind friends who gave the chicken and gravy, the rice and peas, the cakes. Prayers! That's what we need. From these prisoners, locked up in their cold dark cells on Christmas Day, it is incense that ascends into heaven.

Our first two Brothers who dare to serve Christ and the poorest of people: Fr. Hayden Augustine, MOP, and Fr. Brian Kerr, MOP Servitium Dulce Cum Christo Crucifixo.

Chapter Nineteen

....

"See, I have set before you this day life and good,
death and evil. Therefore, choose life, that you and
your descendants way live."

Deut 30:15, 19b

OUR Lord died between two thieves, one good, the other evil. The bad one challenged him, "If you are the son of God, come down from the cross." That was our Lord's last temptation. Had he given in to the pain he suffered, it would have destroyed salvation history and the greatest event ever to happen in our world. Instead, he gave himself over as a sacrifice for love of sinners. This love, carved in our souls, can never die. It is fire in our lives. It bums brightly and enflames us with a desire to serve. Christ's love is our joy: his death for the love of others is the meaning of life.

Jesus hung on the Cross between good and evil. The evil thief, like so many of our friends, tells us to come down from the Cross, come away from the suffering, from old age, poverty, destitution, death. Come away and create for yourself and your loved ones a secure paradise devoid of confusion. Enjoy the best in life: education, house, food, clothes. Jesus would not have done wrong had he come down from the Cross, but he would have come away from suffering and that magnificent act of love for us. The good thief sees Christ as an innocent man and asks, "Please remember me when you go to your kingdom." The good thief recognizes Christ, his goodness, his dreadful suffering, and the majesty of the self-sacrifice. He simply wants to be with Christ in his kingdom.

It is not easy to live in the slums where there are so many thieves. Most people define a thief as an evil man. But for Christ, there is the good thief and the bad thief. God knows, I have met bad thieves: totally selfish men who are bound up with power, who exploit their own poor people, who are violent and arrogant. They damage and destroy women and innocent children and have no sense of responsibility to others. They use others to satisfy themselves. But God also knows, I have met good thieves, and most of the people m the slums are good thieves. I have met such compassion, gentleness, and bold charity, even in destitution. Are many willing to rob? Yes, they are! Are many willing to battle against hunger, starvation, death for the poor? Definitely! Absolutely! I believe if there were enough help, enough people to hang on the Cross with Jesus, in the slums, they would discover with amazement, the beauty of the good thief.

Life is rich with feeling. Good and evil are palpable in the slums. Poverty, dire poverty is there. Yet I experience the resurrection in my life because the Cross of Christ seems to hang high among the Brothers and all who share our works in the slums. The texture of life from day to day is joy and sorrow, despair and hope. So many of the poor are bound up with struggle and tears. They might be swallowed up by the dreadful suffering of poverty which hammers away day after day on their hands and feet. They might become embittered and hardened, and some do, but others joke and laugh as they do whatever work we can offer them. They work, and they serve, and they bring joy to our lives.

Chapter Twenty

....

"Blessed are those who mourn, for they shall be comforted."

Mt 5:4

THERE is a sensuousness to the ghetto yard: women have their breasts hanging out of torn dresses when they bend over cooking and washing. Men and women wash themselves out of doors: with their children watching, they bathe in the yard naked, under moonlight and open skies, standing on a wooden platform under a shower; or they bathe using a washing pan or behind a torn piece of plastic. They sleep and feel each other's flesh pressed against them, four or five piled in one bed. The men urinate in the open carelessly for all to see. Men and women have sex in the same room for their children to hear. All this and nothing to do in the warm tropical night. And the reggae rhythm drives in the night with its clever sensual lyrics, and mock laughter is heard from the crowds who listen so intently.

He held the blade by her neck. "I'll kill you if you tell anybody." Lydia cried and begged for mercy. "Please don't hurt me, daddy, I won't talk." He had forced her to have sex, then sent her off to school. People in the yard laughed and talked: "What an evilous man." But finally they paid it no mind. It is a natural part of ghetto life anyway. One room, one bed, so many bodies: incest, that terrible and unnatural phenomenon, happens. It can't help but happen as the ghetto man has woman

81

after woman, and the woman brings in a new man along with sons and daughters by other men.

When her mother Rose found her Lydia with a big belly, she questioned her. Lydia rested her school books and stripped off her school uniform. "Mama, is pregnant I pregnant? Feel me belly." Rose cried out, "You future gone now. You vomiting?" They clung to each other and wept. Then Rose asked, "Who is the baby father?" Lydia hung her head, "Me no know." Rose took her to the doctor. The doctor was kind. Lydia seemed to know nothing of sex and childbearing.

When he explained, she realized who was the baby father. Lydia didn't want to tell the doctor, but he coaxed it out of her. "You have to register the baby with a father's name." She was silent. "It can't have no name." Silence again. "It is not right for the baby not to carry the name of a father." Lydia told him it was Donnie, her mother's lover. The doctor told Rose, who was full of shame and anger. She knew the type of man Donnie was; she did not chastise her daughter.

Rose told her own sad tale to me: like mother, like daughter. When Rose was a young girl, she had been invited by her uncle to go to Kingston. St. Elizabeth was backward country offering no opportunity to the young. Uncle Philip brought her in when she was thirteen. He sent her to school but wanted her to deal with him. "Him put argument to me. But I told him no, knowing him is me uncle and him have his own wife Hortense and two children." Rose was afraid, for her uncle had a bar and a wholesale nearby. But if he sent her out, she would stop going to school and starve. She didn't want to return to St. Elizabeth for nothing progressive was going on there.

Rose complained to her Aunt Hortense just as Lydia had finally told her mother. "I told Aunt Hortense what was going on. But she didn't back me up. She tell me it was I who was the slack one, and she roughed me up. I found out that I had another auntie in Stand Pipe, and I begged her to take me in. School never work out for me, so I left to help her sell coal and things. Then I worked at Grants Pen for seven years as a maid."

When Rose went to work at Grants Pen. Mrs. Ferguson gave her a bicycle. She used to ride out at night. That's how she met Donnie at the gas station. She told Mrs. Ferguson she was going to church. And at the beginning, she was going to church, but there is no connection between God and ethics in many Christian churches. People are simply told to praise God, clap hands, and love one another. Rose still went to church every now and then for the excitement, even after as a young girl she went and lived with Donnie. Her pastor knew of this, but there was no exactness to his preaching, no right or wrong to this or that action.

After Rose had worked with her for seven years, Mrs. Ferguson went to America. She wanted Rose to go with her, for she cooked and cleaned and hemmed very well, but Rose was pregnant. "If I did go with them, everything would be all right. Rich people know how to treat people right."

Rose knew that even little girls in school uniforms are being harassed by men. They are poor girls who want to go to school. Fathers and uncles have preyed on them. Incest has occurred. More recently, men of means were picking them up in cars. The poor little girls, so vulnerable to vanity, feel good being wanted by older men and receiving money for selling their bodies. Lydia had received money from Donnie, and her mother Rose was promised money by her uncle, if she gave in.

Rose confronted Donnie about the incest. Donnie went into a rage and boxed her until he nearly broke her neck. Then he began to strangle her. The people in the yard cried shame. He used his finger nails and dug a long line in her neck. She showed me the marks. Finally, he cooled down. Mother and daughter lived in fear. Then at last Lydia ran away. That's when Rose came to Faith Centre. "It doesn't matter, Father. When I consider that him would give me just forty dollar now and then, but then him would fight me and take it back. Since Mrs. Ferguson leave, is just two days' work I have, and I even have to provide for him. He himself work as a security guard, but he would rather go to the bar than help. Then him bring in another girl, one after another."

I asked Rose, "Why did you take up with him?"

"Him put argument to me. Him wanted someone him could come home to, and who love him. When I was young, him provide for me."

Lydia took up with a boyfriend. "Him have a room next door," Rose said to me. "Him say I can move in, for now I am his mother."

I gave them a package of food and promised a package a week until they settle down and find jobs. As they walk out our gate, they are arm in arm, abused mother and daughter giving strength and comfort to one another.

Chapter Twenty-One

....

"For I came not to call the righteous but sinners."

Mt 9:13b

CLINKER Samuels is neat, mannerly, courteous, a good little boy. "Why did he shoot the girl? I can't understand it, he never did anything wrong in his life." His mother broke down and cried. Father Hayden allowed her. She wept, head on the desk for a half hour. The girl Candy was only twelve years old. Clinker had gone to collect the partner money from Candy's mother. This was the week when Icilda would pay down for a brand new settee.

Clinker and Candy grew up together in school. He noticed how pretty she was becoming. But she didn't like his awkwardness and rough remarks. He smiled at her. "Look how you getting big. You really getting fat." Candy sucked her teeth and continued reading her comic book. Clinker didn't like her lack of attention. He began pulling her plaits. She sucked her teeth again. He pushed her by the shoulder. "Leave me alone, nuh?" She turned away.

Clinker left. He went into the room of Jacob, a street youth who lived in the yard and who pulled herbs. He saw Jacob's gun on top of the table by the cooking utensils. "What you looking on it for? Try it, nun," goaded Jacob. Clinker picked the gun up and turned it around in his hand. "Anything in it?" Jacob laughed, "The only way you gwine find out is if you try it." Jacob continued frying the salt fish and callaloo.

Clinker brought the gun to Candy. This drew her attention, and she smiled. Clinker said teasingly, "I bet I could shoot you." She replied, "I bet you wouldn't use it." He pulled the trigger twice. Candy fell on the ground, blood on the side of her head.

The Brothers know the boy and his family. Father Hayden patiently followed the case, supported the two sets of parents in their grief, and arranged for a lawyer. All along, he counselled Clinker and accompanied him to court. Today Clinker is in the minimum security home for juvenile offenders in the rural area.

The madness of this random act of murder is hard to understand. Clinker is not evil, not mean, by-nature. Yet it was only because he is a minor, fourteen years, that he was not charged as a violent criminal. As a juvenile, he was charged with manslaughter. His case was helped by the fact that it wasn't Clinker's gun, and there was no serious deliberation and premeditation. Clinker, on an idle dare, wanting the attention of the girl Candy, killed her in an almost playful manner.

Clinker is a little strange, a little odd. He is different from the rest of the street boys. The boy loved old people. He would push old Randolph in the wheelchair, exchange stories and jokes with him, and then bathe him. Clinker loved our retarded residents also. Often after school, he would come among them and play football, wrestle, and skip rope with them. In a word. Clinker loved the outcasts and the broken people that are our homeless. We encouraged him because it was so rare among rough ghetto youth to be gentle of heart.

In his class, the boys called him "Fish" because of his gentleness. This nickname designated him as a homosexual. One day Clinker cried during recess. He flung stones at the other boys and yelled, "I will shoot you." The other boys hollered at him, "Fish, Fish." Clinker began to hate his own gentleness and stopped visiting the old people and retarded. Soon he began boasting about girlfriends he had and his sexual experiences. But then he would switch from his macho-ghetto experience and become sensitive and considerate as he saw our dog Brownie or the stray cats. Forced to be contrary to his own nature. Clinker's personality-switched on and off between Jekyll and Hyde.

He had a deep and genuine hatred for his father Daniel. The old man told Father Hayden, "My seed spread throughout the earth. I have had twenty-four children from twenty-four women." One day, he caught Clinker reading the Bible: "What you doing with this foolishness?" Clinker complained to his mother, but she remained silent. Daniel being a big brute of a man. Moreover, he did give her twenty dollars every now and then.

Icilda spoiled Clinker. For her, he was her special child. He spoke proper English. His clothes were simple but neat; he was reverent to Jesus. She made Clinker into everything his father was not, and his natural gentleness made him malleable in her hands. Clinker often prayed that he would be delivered from the evils of the ghetto. But a gentle boy can hardly survive in the crudeness around him. Occasionally he would let out strange shrieks while asleep. And he would emit odd sounds in the classroom as if to call attention to himself. Then he began giving up his studious habits in school. He wanted to be accepted by the other boys; he wanted to cease being a mama's boy.

What a tragedy! Clinker was not delivered from the evil of his environment. Rather he became a victim of it. Those two bullets through Candy's head sealed it.

How will our Father in heaven regard young Clinker? Somehow He will have mercy: Clinker is a victim and a child of circumstance. The gun was available, and he used it. But woe to those who spread these weapons of violence. God will punish them utterly.

We worship you, we adore you, we give you thanks. There are now 550
Brothers all over the world serving Christ and the poorest of people.

Chapter Twenty-Two

....

"You shall walk after the Lord your God and fear him, and keep his commandments and obey his voice."

Deut 13:4

THERE are three hippopotamuses here at Faith Centre: Mavis, a dainty three hundred and forty pounds; high-chested Mable, three hundred and twenty pounds; Sharon, a tall and muscular two hundred and eighty-pounds.

"Call Sharon." The Amazon came forward. But what a marvellous smile. Dimples on either cheek and one front tooth out.

"What a gwine," she asked humourously, pretending seriousness.

"We need a watchman, someone brutal."

Giggle, giggle, giggle.

"You want me set the other two pon you?"

One big belly laugh.

Sharon is a real Jamaican woman. There is a rock-like strength in her that endures the bludgeoning of ghetto life. She lives with her family on Gold Street. Her father was shot through the head by the police: they thought he was the wanted man Junior Smith when his real name was Junior Stewart. This was the time of the Gold Street massacre. When she visited the morgue, she saw the body tagged Smith.

Today it was laughter, yesterday it was tears. She ran into my office. There was a bloody knife wound slashed across her right arm. "Father, no more sex, no more baby, no more slackness.

I want God. Nothing else. I want to be clean and pure. Lord God, Father, why the man can't leave me alone, is two pickney I have already."

I prayed with her. "Me baby father try force sex on me, but I finish."

Blessed are the persecuted. "You can't give in now. Roland brutalized you and he doesn't take care of the pickney and you. Don't go back."

I called in Roland. "Sharon has changed."

"I realize that."

"You must leave her alone."

"She too feisty."

"If you don't, I'll call the police."

I told all fifteen of our weavers: no more sex, no more children. "Sex with man after man, with or without children is animal. Abstinence, pure and simple." So many had fallen into the trap: maybe this man will help me, another baby, another battle, lashings, screaming, black eyes, jail. But the flesh called out again—another man, another baby, another man again.

None of the women on our weaving project has had any children over the past two years. They have picked up the pieces of their lives and taken responsibility, alone; they must be mother and father to their children. I have seen dignity come to their lives, and with it, laughter, friendship, and self-respect. They have had to gain self-control over so many appetites and in turn take charge of their own destiny. At the foot of the Cross, they have laid their loneliness, their poverty, and the struggles of everyday life, these marvellous daughters of God.

I called Sharon, not to be a guard, but a guardian. She was to inspect the shacks in the neighbourhood, to look for the bodies on the sides of streets, to watch out for those who are hungry. Unarmed, she was to guard against death.

"Yes, Father, I love that work."

Sharon helps us do whatever we can for the people—soup, shelter, repair of shacks, medical aid, showers for those with no water, clothes for the naked. Hunger, sickness, malnutrition, deprivation come in the form of people, dead but that they walk. All this suffering, but it brings us no despair. It is more the pepper and vinegar of everyday life.

Sharon is thoughtless about her own welfare.

"What makes you happy, Sharon?"

"Serving my people, serving God."

Yesterday there were tears, today there is laughter. The other two hippos came and sat on my desk. More belly laughs.

"Fadda, we gwine help. We unionized, we ina it too."

More cackles and belly laughs.

How are these daughters of God going to ascend into heaven unless the Lord uses a crane and pulleys to haul them up?

Father forgive me, for I have sinned.

Chapter Twenty-Three

. . . .

*"These all look to thee, to give them their food in
due season."*

Ps 104:27

WHOMP! Whomp! Whomp!
All heads turned, those of Black vendors and atten-
dants as well as those of White tourists, as this spectacle
descended the road at Dunns River Falls: Mavis, Sharon, and
Mable, three elephants from our weaving shop, weighing easily half a ton among them. Following them were thirteen other
weavers and workers, including three slender men, our slim
driver, and one White woman. Everyone was carrying something: bags, towels, huge pots of chicken and rice and peas,
igloos with ice and drinks, and more.

Down, down, down the steps descended our Faith Centre
constellation, right to the foot of the falls. Then with no shyness
or sense of ill-ease, they proceeded to appropriate all three pic-
nic tables next to the falls. Imagine! Every visitor coming down
the stairs would see, first, not the falls but our illustrious group
from the slums of Kingston.

It all came about when the weavers heard we were taking the
residents of Faith Centre for a beach outing. They ganged up
on one of our volunteers. "Miss Grace, what about we for the
beach? When we a go?"

"How about next week Thursday?" Hoorays went up all
around.

"The next thing: where we a go?"

"Dunns River Falls," exclaimed several weavers.

"Are you serious? With all the tourists?"

"We will be Black Jamaican tourists."

That Thursday, our big truck made the journey to Ocho Rios with this bevy of ghetto women and men. The entire trip was charged with excitement. One of our elephants went sailing to the floor at a sharp turn. Round after round of songs were offered. Jokes were exchanged. Food was consumed with relish. "We going foreign. We going foreign."

At the foot of the falls, weavers and workers tackled the first serious order of business: lunch. Enormous quantities of food were uncovered and dished out. Elephants don't get to be elephants with a likkle bit of food! Curious tourists leaned over the railing above the group with questions about what was being served. "Chicken, rice and peas," twanged the reply, totally-unintelligible to the visitors from abroad.

After lunch, the group separated into clusters and seriously and in great detail began to scrutinize each and every visitor who had come to climb the falls. Lengthy-discussions ensued about hair styles, fashions, scantiness of swim suits, colour, size, and shape of people. Then suddenly everyone got very excited. Fingers wagged rapidly.

"Look! Mongoloid, mongoloid!"

True enough, below our weavers was a gathering of White people, all, apparently, mentally retarded, including several Down's syndrome youngsters. Our weavers and workers are used to being with mentally handicapped people, but they had never seen any in white skins before. They were curious and delighted. "That one favours Harold. The other one favours Garth. And that one favours Frankie." Not satisfied just to look, some of the weavers went up to the group, introduced them-selves, shook hands, laughed, and joked.

No one would climb up the falls, not even the men. But everyone made the journey right to the bottom of the falls and leaned up against the rocks with water crashing down around them. Sharon climbed up a tree and stretched out for a nap. Tony took pictures of all our bathing beauties. Mable looked like leviathan emerging from under the falls. Juliette, Ann Marie, and Rosie romped in the water: "Be baptized in the name of the Lord."

Finally, time to go home. Everyone agreed, for it had been a full day. Back in the truck now, they polished off the remaining food. Not a scrap of food returned to Kingston. Then, one by one, nearly everyone fell into a deep, satisfied sleep. Mable spread a blanket on the floor of the truck and cotched another blanket under her head and covered up with another. Juliette's head bobbed up and down in drowsiness until at last she curled up like an innocent lamb on the floor next to Mable. Not until the truck reached Higholborn Street did the group come alive again, and then they all proudly proclaimed to the community, "We don't need to go foreign. Dunns River Falls is better than foreign!"

Of course, Dunns River Falls may never be the same after this invasion!

Guests going to the wedding of Cathy and Mike.

Chapter Twenty-Four

....

"It shall come to pass in the latter days
that the mountain of the house of the Lord
shall be established as the highest of the mountains,
and shall be raised above the hills; and
all the nations shall flow to it,
and many people shall come, and say:
'Come, let us go up to the mountain of the Lord,
to the house of the God of Jacob;
that he may teach us his ways
and that we may walk in his paths.'"

Is 2:2-3

CATHY and Mike are getting married. All kinds of excitement. The Down's syndrome residents are cleaning the chapel: they are bouncing and chatting away in their special language. Frankie is doing a balancing act with chairs on his head! But his pants are falling off so he has to reach down to pull them—OOPS! Down come the chairs. Wayne is wheeling around the bucket with the mop in it and singing his monotone love song. Harold, lazy as ever, is standing around, arms folded as if he is some supervisor giving orders. He winks at me as I go over and tell Ricky and Dwane how to pack the chairs. When I tell him to work he shakes my hand. You can't win!

This morning I appeared at my breakfast table at home only to see three huge women demolishing the Brothers' breakfast of eighteen eggs and mounds of sardines. It was meant to serve twenty people, but these three giantesses thought otherwise.

The Brothers had to go back to the kitchen and cook again. We will also have to skimp the next week to make sure we can balance our budget.

Curry goat. They really are making a case for it. Legs apart, coal burning, frying pan sizzling, and all sorts of excited chatter. "We gwine fatten up Cathy. Right now she is like pickney chile: when we done feed her tonight, she gwine look like woman."

"Taste it, nuh, Father?" They cackled a raucous laugh when the pepper burnt me. "Cho, you is a chiney man, you too soft."

Bruce and Maggie got the tables and chairs. Mary made the cakes and cooked the chicken. Sr. Mary made cakes and drinks for four hundred people. Diana had to get her hand in it too: salad and more cake. Everybody chipped in something so the bride and groom would not have to pay any cost. It was busy, busy all day long.

This was our first-ever wedding at Faith Centre. It was jam-packed for this couple. Our chapel is used for a night shelter and since the hurricane it has been housing other homeless people as well. Beds, bed pans, walking sticks, clothes had to be moved out. Then we had to decorate with secondhand clothes all these homeless people fit for a wedding.

The chapel was transformed with balloons, streamers, flowers. Our homeless residents, our church people, our ghetto women and men were the invited guests. Then there were the parents of the bride and groom who came from Canada and the United States. Also our local volunteers.

What a marvellous thing! Blacks, Whites, Chinese, Indians, young and old, beggars, professional men and women, the broken, the healthy: all united in this joyous event. The music was lustily sung by all. Deaf and dumb Carl had a great big grin on his face during the whole service, as if he heard the music.

The bride and groom were nicely dressed, but no long dress and no three-piece suit. Their spirits soared along with the congregation. And the singers from our concert group gave a rousing gift—their talent—joined in by all: "Rejoice My Soul."

In the stream of activities that go on from day to day at Faith Centre, it is good to pause for a while and enjoy the beauty of our people. Mike had visited Faith Centre nearly three years ago. In his gentle manner he asked, "May I be of any help at Faith Centre?" Three times Cathy has come to offer her nursing skills. Both sent by God on a mission, not knowing each other, but sharing that one desire to be of service to our poor and homeless. They have met and are now married. Christ is the centre of their lives, filling them with a deep desire to contribute to his mission and his work. With their eyes on him, they met and are now bound together in him. What a mystery! That Divine Providence drawing people, total strangers, together and offering them His abounding love and uniting people who would otherwise have been alien to each other.

What an amalgamation of people God congregates. He seems to me an off-beat God, full of surprises, full of mystery. God draws us to Himself in the poor and binds us together in the Cross. This is our joy!

This little flower is strange and beautiful in the garden of God.

Chapter Twenty-Five

"So then you are no longer strangers and sojourn-
ers, but you are fellow citizens with the saints and
members of the household of God, built upon the
foundation of the apostles and prophets, Christ Jesus
himself being the cornerstone, in whom the whole
structure is joined together and grows into a holy
temple in the Lord; in whom you also are built into it
for a dwelling place of God in the Spirit."

Eph 2:19-22

GOD, His heavenly kingdom, His eternal home, and the unutterable beauty and power of His presence and love: I want people to know Him as our community of Brothers does. Because we want to bring the laity to Christ the Bridegroom, we engage lay people in our works with the poor and destitute. It is the poor who reveal Christ to us and to the laity. Lay people are stirred to sympathy with the crucified Christ in the least of our brothers and sisters, and they want to discover the Christ so mysteriously present in the poor. It is the Christ in them responding to the words of Jesus in the poor that makes them desirous of helping us in our ministries.

Our laity see the terrible desecration of life in our poor brothers and sisters, and they desire to do something for them. Compassion is the Christ stirred in our laity, a feeling and emotion, which is the deepest part of our humanity. In fact, it crosses over into the very divine instinct in us to love, to live, to die for others, so profoundly exemplified in the life of

Jesus and so deeply in us all who are by blood and spirit united with Christ.

What a tremendously generous people Jamaicans are. There are thousands who do small as well as large favours, who give small sums as well as large sums. They give, and they give, without end, and our poor are thereby lifted up to the Lord. And there are many, many lay people from abroad, indeed all over the world, who not only give generously but who come and visit and work with the least of our brothers and sisters.

Beloved friends among the laity: they are serious men and women with leadership and a spirit of total dedication who have surrendered themselves to this work and purpose. And they do this without any material gain or support from our religious community. All is done from the spirit of God within seeking the spirit of God without. They have an inexhaustible love for the Lord, and they know it, and they obey this command of Christ, "As you did it to one of the least of these my brethren, you did it to me."

Our laity turn to Christ in the poor. They desire union with him. They desire to serve him as humble servants. They desire peace in the heart. Extraordinarily varied, they humbly serve the Lord with their many gifts.

The laity are like our garden, and our garden is full of flowers. All turn to the sunlight and blow with the gentle and sometimes strong winds of the Holy Spirit. They make our lives radiant, beautiful, and, occasionally, complex. They are so plural, so colourful, and so lovely as they are; and they awaken our sense of joy as we work with the wounds of our broken poor.

I see our lay people turning to Christ, walking the journey towards Christ, discovering the depth of their true selves wherein Christ lives. I am so happy when I see them joyfully giving themselves for an inner self they did not know existed—a richness of personhood—indeed, a divine life within that goes past selfishness, self-concern, and existence in a purely material world.

As the Brothers turn to Christ the Light of Lights, we want our laity to turn to him also. Together we will walk the road of life, struggling together towards that brilliant Son, warmed by his love and message, "Come and follow me." I have preached to thousands, even tens of thousands in Jamaica and overseas. We have sung to thousands too. The message is always the same: "Follow him. Walk with him. Die to self, and live for him. Go the road of Calvary, and there you will find Christ and happiness."

We want to bring many there. It is a hard road to travel, but it is the purpose of our existence. As we live our lives and do our works with the poor, as we turn our faces to Christ on Calvary, we thank God that so many have joined us and that many more will come as pilgrims, walking with the Cross.

Everyday, the miracle of the feeding of the five thousand.

Chapter Twenty-Six

·························

*"Go into the ark, you and all your household; . . .
every living thing that I have made I will blot out
from the face of the ground."*

Gen 7:1a, 4b

WINSTON strides bare-backed, sweat gleaming black in the hot noonday sun. This son of the ghetto is a tall prince, powerfully built with square shoulders and slim hips. He never wears a shirt or a smile, or shoes, but only old cut-off trousers. In the street Winston strolls upright, cool and easy, in full possession of himself, without haste, neither turning to the left nor to the right, his head—the crown of his body—lifted high and dignified.

"Election finished, but war no done. Come, I want to show you something." We walked along Barry Street onto Gold Street without a further word exchanged. The personality of the ghetto roads and yard exuded waste: the youths and the adults slouched on sidewalks, half-asleep, idly chatting, hanging loose in bars, dulled by music sound systems and sedated by alcohol and drugs. Not even the higglers and market women seemed intent on sales, and the John crows glided and landed without energy on old dumps and garbage heaps gone stale. Skinny dogs with skeleton ribs and patches of mange walked sniffling the bilge water that lazily ran along the side-street gutters. Circling slowly on bicycles some youths inertly pulled on spliffs and cigarettes behind dark glasses. The ghetto seemed as languid as mindless matter.

Winston ambled on, I, a few paces behind. He brought me to the two-room shack, now half broken-down and in complete confusion. Cocaine invaders-creatures of night—had ransacked Winston's shack. His baby mother, Kathleen, a tall, pretty, light-skinned ghetto girl whom he called his "princess," had fled. Their four little children, two boys, two girls, had locked themselves in the bedroom.

"Two years it take to build up this little ranch. All my work mash up. All my tools gone. Is like an evil spirit come from the belly of the earth and move everything away.

"My intention is a castle, for me and me woman and pickney. I not a beggar. It not ina me. I will rebuild it with my own hands."

Amazingly, Winston was not angry. Calmly, quietly, he picked up the pieces of broken chairs and table. The torn sheet and clothes he gathered and folded like a woman. This ghetto man is macho, but his mother is in him also. He heated the leftover porridge for the children. "Come, eat." The smallest girl wept. "You mama gone? She soon come." He explained that she is not hurt. The ghetto people knew she must be down at Aunt Maude's, where she kept two children she had by a previous baby father named Lester.

"I want you to help me with the lost tools. If you can, fine; if you can't, so it go. But I mostly want to check you with what I think. This is a different appointed time. In time past, people poor because them have no employment. Now them poor because them unemployable. This is a different generation born of the seed of the dragon. The dragon in the book of Revelation sow a new idea in poor people's brains. My people used to think 'I poor but I must be good.' Now them think 'I poor and I can be badder than the rest.'"

Winston told me that the boy who invaded his place is named Cork Screw. He is short and thick and can't stay at one place. Cork Screw is always on the move. His eyes never look on one thing; they shift from thing to thing, from person to person. When he stands, his fingers are always twitching. "Him hot, Father. Him always look like him looking something to tief or like police a run him down." Winston's intelligence was unguided by proper schooling, but the intelligence was nevertheless there. He saw things clearly, and he had vibes.

"A detective study will show you Cork Screw come through the backyard where the toilet is, and him fling my tools over the zinc fence where a boy with whom him spar wait and catch them.

"Anybody fidgety when him need coke. At times a man go crazy, like ants a bite him, or hammer a nail on the nerves.

"I gwine bide me time. I gwine cool it. Trouble mustn't trouble trouble."

I asked, "Why not report it to the police?" The reply was short. "Police out of the runnings."

Winston continued, "Only if the police clamp them to a height will things change. And that would take more police than we have people."

This island is spoiled like a blighted mango. We are a young nation, but we are force-ripened by the single controlling thought of sharing the big apple: the American dream. It is weird, odd, out of order, impossible, and finally destructive. Our fruit is no more than a blackie mango, not an orange pumped up by fertilizer.

Winston announced, "As I see it, evil is stationary right now. It is boss. That is why Noah build an ark; corruption set in. Me no know how it come or where it go. I don't know how to leave it behind.

"A little ranch is what I want. That's my boat. There I gwine keep my family, two goats, two pigeons, and two cows."

Kathleen suddenly threw the zinc gate open. "Them kill Cork Screw. Them catch him when him and Blackie bruk in a man's shop."

Winston smiled. It was not a happy smile, but one of resignation. "Me love me poor people, but everything gone sour."

Chapter Twenty-Seven

"Whoever causes one of these little ones who
believe in me to sin, it would be better for him to have
a great millstone fastened round his neck and to be
drowned in the depth of the sea."

Mt 18:6

MANY of our ghetto people were simple country folk;
they trusted in nature, they trusted their neighbours,
they trusted God. The attitude of trust inborn from birth is
not easy to remove. This childlike openness to everything
and everyone is like Adam and Eve in paradise before the fall.
Christianity, the benevolence of the good earth, the love of one
another in village life: all these conspire to promote an innocence in the Jamaican soul; no one intends to hurt anyone.

The simplicity of rural life, which is the root of the Jamaican
psyche, is both simple and profound. Everything and everyone
is considered good. There is naughtiness, but merely as spice,
not the substance of daily life. As the country folk know it, God
and man provide for even the least of the brethren. The birds
of the air, the animals in the fields, and the lush fruitful nature
care for one and all.

But the point of rupture is politics, radio and television, and
the traffic which flows from country to city and back. The hard-
driving deejay and dance hall music, the pseudo-American
DJ voice in the media, the hard-sell on material goods: these
inject a restlessness in the soul of simple country people. And
they cannot stay in the stillness of the night talking simple talk,

sharing fruits, and worshipping God. The fascination of the city is not less powerful than a magnet drawing a weaker body irresistibly toward itself.

Country folk are awkward fools: this is the fallacious assumption of both the urban and rural people. Urban people, ghetto or otherwise, are slick and wise to the pleasures and goods of the world. They arc modern and have the smarts to juice out what's to be gotten out of this life.

And so the swarms of simple rural people fly to honey in Kingston, only to find a bitter and destructive poison. The ethics of the city is dog-eat-dog. Everyman exists for himself and no one else. However, those from the country have within themselves only that attitude of simple trust. They are exploited to the last, not knowing that everything and everyone is up for grabs. And the sacredness of life and people is not the governing principle in life. To survive in the city, anything goes. Money is hard to come by, and the benevolence once offered by nature and people has to be replaced by an uncompromising attitude of salesmanship and deceit in order to survive. One's labour, one's talent, one's moral integrity are quickly degraded in a competitive world. Whatever a person can sell, he or she sells: cocaine, ganja, his or her body. It's a fast world in which life is a dollar and love is sex.

City life in the urban ghetto is worth nothing, yet it is the heart of modern life. It is where the world is going: toward cities without a soul. But kinetic energy is high, and sheer energy— frenzied and unemotional, wild and senseless as a mechanical pin-ball machine—gives an illusion of excitement. To smell the grass and to dip one's feet in a cool running stream is too country. That is for people who don't know the excitement of furious energy and an imagination released from the boredom of everyday life.

Politics! This is the power principle for many of our urban ghetto people. This is when one can contest and forget oneself; this is when life is free and full of dangerous excitement; this is when competition is nerve-racking and the field is limited only by the boundaries of the island. Cheering, jeering, and laughing, our people get into the arena, and then pushing, shoving, yelling, stoning, and killing, win the ball game under their captains, the political leaders.

It's actually fun! And even if it costs hundreds of lives, it has been a high: from the screaming microphones right down to the guns and bullets that drive our people behind walls and bars. Excitement—tragic or joyous—it doesn't matter: a good time was had by all.

But Jamaica! Sweet Jamaica! How can we exploit the innocence of our simple people, poor and trusting and ready to believe every charismatic and evangelical politician who promises salvation which can only be gained with labour and self-sacrifice. Our people are simple and childlike; not stupid and senseless, but simple in a trusting sense. They believe in people, they believe in the goodness of politicians, they will follow leaders, as if paradise had not been lost and that it need be regained by the sweat of our brow.

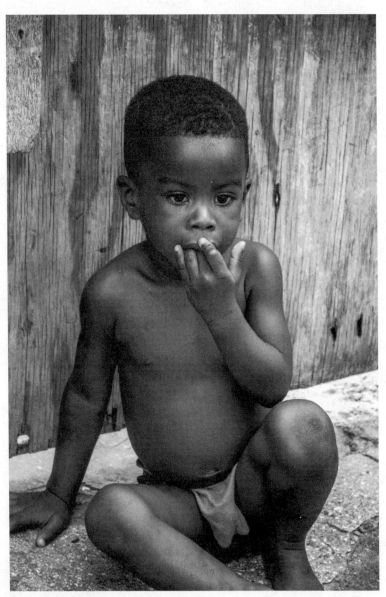

What's my future? I love the Brothers.

Chapter Twenty-Eight

"Fallen, fallen is Babylon the great! It has become a dwelling place of demons, a haunt of every foul spirit."

Rev 18:2

"GUNMAN a come! Lord God in heaven." Crowds scattered on either side of the street, driven as if a tidal wave had swept down the middle of Heroes Circle. The posse strode towards Stephens Street. People screamed and jumped over fences; others fled across Heroes Circle. Down came the vigilantes, full of malice, menacing with guns in hand and in pocket. Their shoulders were high, like those of commanders of armies. They rode through the streets with pride, proclaiming their terrible intentions. One shot in the air, the gun—his bugle—in hand. They were masters of darkness and death. They had folly imbibed the lessons of the evil one.

Some of these men laughed as they saw the poor people scatter like rabbits. They enjoyed their authority as masters do over servants in a place of wickedness. They reviled their own poor people and the servility imposed by terror. Power, the taste of it, how sweet! Even though they themselves were dispossessed and powerless in their own ghetto lives and it was dominance over their own poor, it was delicious. These were the new lords of evil, top ranking kings of darkness, inherited from a politics of retribution in the recent history of our island.

Roland was in bed. "I tired, I want sleep," he told Mel. "I gwine lay down a little while." His old granny had gone out to wash some clothes. Valerie had left that morning to visit her sister to borrow some money. Roland had helped James that morning and afternoon two days before the election to nail some wood to build his new house. James had nowhere to live, and he captured a little space that the other families in the yard did not use.

Roland flopped into bed. The little children flopped into bed with him. They loved Roland. Although he was sixteen years old and had big strong shoulders, he was not like other men. He liked little children, and he often lifted them gently on his shoulders or he would whirl them around in a circle faster and faster, till they got dizzy and fell down laughing in ecstasy.

When the gunmen came, he was asleep. The little children heard the gun shots and the shouting, but Roland was fast asleep. The mothers and young adults ran into their rooms and grabbed their little children. Little Maisie screamed when her mother was suddenly confronted by seven gunmen. "Get her out of here." One shoved the mother and child aside.

Roland jumped out of sleep and under the bed. "Get out of there." Silence. "I say, get out from under the bed." Silence. They threw the little bed out the door. Then they picked up Roland and slapped him. "Why you don't answer when big man talk to you?" They slapped him again and again. He whimpered. Then the leader placed the gun by his ear and shot him. Little Maisie ran away from her mother and screamed, "Roland." The gang leader kicked her. Maisie flew back to her mother.

They left, but not before having inserted sadness and terror in the hearts of all those in the yard. Outside, they set fire to a little shack. Shanti, a little old coolie woman, lived there. Thank God she was not inside. They burnt it down and yelled to everyone, "Remember. Is I a rule." The people brought water and tried to put out the fire but not in time.

James came up to me this morning. "I want to pray with you. Father. I feel sorrow. The little boy dead. Him is an innocent. Him do no harm to nobody." I prayed with James. "But I also want to pray in thanksgiving. No harm was done to me." He explained, "The gang came up to me yard. One said outside my door, 'Make we do a thing.' Another said, 'No, man, no.' The other replied, 'We can cook a man inside.' 'No.' Praise God, is because I worship me God I alive today."

I asked James why the gang came. His reply: "We is PNP. A policeman shot a JLP who had a gun that morning right outside the yard. Is revenge, Father."

Election 1993 is over. It was peaceful in general. For that we must all give thanks. The politicians worked hard to promote peace. Everyone possible was mobilized to bring peace. But is the word enforce not a more accurate word? I am glad that peace happened, enforced or not. But there were policemen everywhere. JDF men everywhere. Helicopters patrolled all night long, plain-clothes police with guns roamed the streets. That's what brought about peace.

We must look at these things realistically. What occurred during the election was tantamount to a police state: law enforced, violence threatened in order to keep the peace. We must also face these facts: there are many guns around, drugs are everywhere, vigilantes and posses are in the ghettoes. This island is riddled with poverty and with violence. It is the disease of this nation. It is the sickness of our country, this country we all love so much, this country we must struggle for.

A physician is needed to prescribe the remedy and to apply it, no matter what the cost.

Akcee, the most delicious food grown in Jamaica for "Running Boat."

Chapter Twenty-Nine

"For he delivers the needy when he calls,
the poor and him who has no helper.
From oppression and violence he redeems their life;
and precious is their blood in his sight."

Ps 72:12, 14

VIOLENCE is like cancer in the stomach. It must be uprooted from our land. It must yield to the physician's knife. But to root it out, we must know its causes. I maintain that today perhaps the greatest cause of our violence is no longer politics, but consumerism. First politics, now consumerism has sown a deadly sickness into the hearts and minds of Jamaica people.

A major furniture store still tells people, "You can be a millionaire." In a country which is made up primarily of poor people, this is dangerous. Most of our poor people of today were born poor and will die poor. The point of this advertisement— "You can be a millionaire"—and many other advertisements is that they make our people dream of what they will never have. The purpose of such wanton and irresponsible advertising is to stir people's appetites so that they desire goods attainable only by the rich, goods totally beyond the humble wages and capabilities of the poor.

Nor do the poor have the discriminating powers to say, "I should put education, food, and housing above expensive furniture and colour television." The poor are simple people, many from the rural parts, who trust people's words and statements, even when it is mere advertisement. Advertisements, on the other hand, prey upon our fleshy nature and our desire for pleasure and the satisfaction of our every instinct.

Poor people believe they'll be happy if they have expensive consumer goods. They don't know better, and they are only human. Consumer goods can be seen behind glass windows, on shelves, driven in the streets—everywhere, telling everyone, "Buy me." All manner of goods are advertised and promoted for sale. Whether we possess such goods—and no one doubts that many Jamaicans have the best you can get in America—or whether we only see such goods advertised and for sale, they have created an impact. The goods are desired, they are willed. It is almost a law of life: what we see is what we want. And the poor want what they see and cannot have.

For the poor, this creates frustration and un-happiness. They buy what they cannot afford, obtaining the money through theft, drug trafficking, or endless hours of labour and savings. At the counter, no one is going to ask where the money came from. Many of our ghetto people have colour televisions, refrigerators, brand new furniture, and the latest in clothes. The men wear heavy metal necklaces; the women dye their hair—yellow, purple, blue, pink.

When the poor cannot get what they have been seduced into wanting, their frustration turns into anger, and the anger leads to violence. They lie, they steal, they kill. They hate themselves. They hate others. They perpetrate crimes so as to possess the goods they desire. They take drugs in order to separate themselves from the ugliness of their everyday life. They hallucinate—with or without drugs—creating a candy-coloured and rainbow dream which momentarily allows them to escape the reality of their day-to-day straggles.

DIARY OF A GHETTO PRIEST 119

These acts of our poor people are wrong: that is truth not to be denied. But I believe the greater guilt lies in those who refuse to face up to the implications of the goods they sell, the values they spread, and the advertisements they beam as principles of life in a poor nation's psyche. It is clear that violence and consumerism are bound as one. We need to take this seriously.

We need a new era of responsible business. We need to ask: what are appropriate goods and appropriate advertisements? How can we condone liberal consumerism when we are a nation that can barely survive? We have a deplorable school system, a public health care system in near shambles, few jobs with miserly pay, and almost a total lack of family life. We must have some self-definition economically. We must be discerning and slowly build an appropriate lifestyle for our people in line with the economy of the greater part of our population. If we don't, America will be our self-definition. Pretending to be Miami, we will be a schizophrenic country: split between who we are and who we aspire to be.

Fr. Hayden teaching ghetto kids about peace. He is one of our first members.

Chapter Thirty

....

"Sheol has enlarged its appetite
and opened its mouth beyond measure;
and the nobility of Jerusalem and her
multitude go down."

Is 5:14

ON Heroes' Day we had a marvellous evening. That morning we decided to "run boat"—cook up a big oil drum of food. We threw everything in it: mutton bones, beef bones, loads of green bananas, yams, cho-cho, dumplings, cock soup flavourings, Pickapeppa sauce, country peppers, scallions and onions. Under the drum we shoved sticks, newspaper, and old pieces of wood. We sat around the fire, all eighty of us, people from the ghetto. Brothers, and a few benefactors. We laughed and talked, played a little music, and ate a belly full. One fat woman said, "Better to make belly burst than throw 'way food." So we licked the platter clean!

Then we prayed and chatted and laughed about old times. We made up a song:

> Put down your guns, my brothers,
> Put down your guns, my sisters.
> Put down your guns,
>   we are friends, not enemies,
> One in the Lord.
> God gives to every person,
> Love is going to heal us all

These are memories of great joy and simplicity shared in Christian unity. It is what makes life worth living. And, it is truly Jamaican. Beautiful and simple and so very gentle. The wit was marvellous and down-to-earth. There was great mutual understanding.

By nature Jamaicans love people. We are no European existentialists who find hell in other people: rather we find God in even person. But we have lost the vision of a good island people living simply but comfortably, struggling towards nationhood, with our reality to become what we were meant to be: out of many, one people under God!

Swiss psychologist Carl Jung, arguably one of the greatest thinkers of our century, says that a religious outlook is necessary for psychic health. He reports that in his thirty years of treating patients in the second half of life, that is, over thirty-five years of age, every one of them had fallen ill because he or she had lost that which the living religions in every age have given: a meaning for life. Every human being searches for some insight into what it means to be a human being. We search for whatever keeps us growing into the deeply centred, loving human beings God made us to be.

In the Jamaica of today, we have defined the meaning of life in consumerist and materialistic terms, not in terms of love and care for one another and centredness on God. We are convinced that if we can provide jobs, money, and goods for every ghetto person, we will have peace. But we have forgotten what St. Augustine says: "Our hearts are restless until we rest in God." Our search for God in materialism is fatal; mammon can never be God. And, as Albert Camus says, the consequence of living in a free democratic world of moneymaking without God is total isolation from one another. A person must learn to live alone since it is too difficult to live with others. Individual concerns and differences compel one to live alone. In such a situation, as is quickly happening in Jamaica as we lose our sense of community, "A person who has learned how to remain alone with his suffering has little left to learn." But the tragedy is that we need to learn that "There is but one truly serious problem, and that is judging whether life is or is not worth living."

The face of this nihilistic existentialism in Jamaica is often violence. We live in the tropics, we live with each other in the streets, but we carry guns and knives. In our alienation, every man is presumably an enemy. At the heart of it, life is not worth much. Life is cheap, both ours and that of others. We will kill or be killed.

Being poor or austere, feeling hunger and rain falling through the roof, not having shoes or underwear, having to study in the night by candle light: none of these experiences because of lack of job and money can measure up to the terrible suffering of loneliness, abandonment, and isolation which is so severely inflicted on the poor, and even on our middle and upper classes. Poverty need not lead to lovelessness or violence, certainly not in the Christian faith, but we are afflicted because we have defined the dignity of life according to a false standard.

Individualism has set in, alienation has begun.

Who will lead me; who will guide me? I seek the Lord.

Chapter Thirty-One

....

"Father, forgive them; for they know not what they do."

Lk 23:34

RUDDY has grown into a handsome boy, tall and broad-shouldered. Often a smile would break across his square face: a flash of a smile lights on his smooth black face. He was going daily to a gym on East Queen Street preparing himself for that big break. "Mike McCallum, watch my dust. I'm going to be King." He would dance around me and jab as he did some shadow boxing. "Wait till I become a millionaire. I'm going to give you everything you need for the poor people."

In the first fight, he was flattened; in the second, he almost ran out of the ring. This time the old confidence was back, but in came Hurricane Gilbert. This time, it was his father Oswald who got knocked out. Ruddy said his father got a massive heart attack and died. Ruddy's fight had to be cancelled.

"Is it a sin. Father? I have no feeling that my father died."

"You can't force feelings. Ruddy. But you must bury him with respect, even if without feelings."

No one cried, none of the three daughters, nor the two sons; nor did his wife Emelda: "He did nothing good by us. All he did was use us. The only inheritance he has is his three daughters made into prostitutes, a mad wife, and sons who have no love for him.

"I will pray for him," said Emelda, "and say nothing bad about him to the children, but I have nothing but bitterness in my heart. The little girl Gwendoline he made pregnant can cotch in the bed where he slept with her. I am not going back. I want nothing to do with anything he was associated with.

"Watch over Ruddy, Father. He is a young boy and a good boy. He needs guidance."

On the night of the nine-night, I could hear the chanting. What a forgiving people Jamaicans are! Even Emelda was there, and the three daughters and Ruddy. Over and over they sang in long droning voices, "The Lord is my Shepherd, I'll not want. He maketh me down to lie." There was weeping, even among the daughters. "Forgive us, Lord, and forgive our father. All of us are unworthy servants." They were wrapped in each other's arms. Emelda in the meanwhile stood in the shadows silently, clutching a handkerchief. Sadness and bitterness passed through her, and finally forgiveness.

She told Ruddy, "He didn't know better. But you must not be like him. You must be a child of your mother, not your father."

Back to training and shadow boxing. But Ruddy soon gave up. He wasn't mean enough. His coach told him he had to hate his opponent, and it just wasn't in Ruddy. He hadn't the killer instinct. Perhaps if he had truly hated his father, but it was more indifference, not hatred he had for Oswald.

"Ruddy, that's the fifth thing you have given up." I was stem with him. "First you start up in school; you dropped out because of lack of interest. Then it was mechanics, but you stopped going to the garage. Next it was welding, but you found it too demanding. Even in the gardening, you lose patience and drift away."

"One more time, Father."

"You don't stick to anything."

"Don't say that, Father."

"I mean it. I don't think you can stick to anything."

Ruddy's clothes have become fashionable, not those of a poor slum boy, but stylish ganzie, blue jeans, runners, a brand new watch, darkers. I told him not to see me until he straightened out what he wants in life. I could tell that self-control, hard work, steadiness, patience, and austerity were not in him. He would skid through life, doing things by accident rather than purpose, and get nowhere. Ruddy could not take anything seriously. He could not afford to take anything seriously since he had no inner self, no belief that he could get anything done. There was no substance within, no foundation on which to build, block by block, a life that is significant. He would not contribute to the well-being of other people's lives or of his own.

*   *   *

I love Ruddy as my own son. For seven years he has been around with the Brothers. There is no evil in him: he doesn't steal, he doesn't disobey, and he is not rude. But I cannot get to the centre of his being. I cannot make him into a serious young man. What is this missing centre? It's that inner substance, that inner stability, a sense of self that comes from being loved, being dealt with seriously, being chastised and encouraged. Parents must take responsibility for a child and shape his morality, his experience, his attitude of mind. Ruddy was born as an accident, not out of love, and he just happened to be around the house as far as his father was concerned. He was not rooted in a father's love. For a boy, a mother's love is just not enough; a man must teach him a man's ways. Not only physically, but psychologically and spiritually, a boy needs a close identity with his father, as docs a girl with her mother.

This is the major problem in the Jamaican psyche: the missing male, the unstable male. Many Jamaican boys grow up in the ghetto without a father's care. Males are temporary in the life of ghetto women. They come and they go. Jamaica may be said to be a fatherless nation since there is hardly a home among the poor where there has been a responsible man. In Ruddy's case there was a father, but there was no parenting, no values passed on nor skills nor education, no connection between the son and the father.

Love takes stability and brings about stability. If it were a matter of economics being the main problem in Jamaica's men being so unstable, then one would expect the girls and women of our society also to be unstable and irresponsible. But this is not so: our poor ghetto women are marvellous and strong, stable and enduring. Give a ghetto woman a job to be done, and it will be done. She will steal, maybe, but she will get the job done. Poverty, then, is not the cause of the troubled male in Jamaica.

Our men are capable of energy. They will pour themselves out with reckless abandon in work and in play. But then they must move on. They do not establish lasting relationships with women or with children. Nor will they stay with a job that requires repetition, steadiness, tenacity. There is big money, a big job, and momentary excitement. Everything is spent now, at the moment in some debauched activity or for some object way beyond the means of a poor man.

There is despair at the heart of the Jamaican ghetto male. He doesn't believe he can attain anything: he doesn't believe he can succeed in any relationship. Nothing is worthwhile but the intensity and pleasure offered at the given moment. Therefore, why take care of the small things of everyday life? Why save money? Why repair things? The ghetto male has seen one father figure after another in his life, if he has seen any. He has moved from one rented shack to another. School, church, teachers, preachers shift in and out of his life without meaning and without success. There is food today, but none tomorrow. He lives with a new sister and brother in the family, depending on who is the new male in his mother's life. Cousins seek temporary shelter with his mother. Things change so fast and so often to the young ghetto male that nothing and no one seems reliable. Nothing is stable, nothing is permanent, nothing is lasting. So why not seize the moment: spend the money you have, buy the best, grab whatever pleasure is at hand, laugh and make merry. There is no meaning but now, no value to life but pleasure.

That's the way his father was. What I try to teach Ruddy is the opposite: patience and hard work. But he leaves the Brothers and goes home. We can't win. All we can do is to deliver Ruddy into the hands of God. If he matures into being a good young man, it will only be by God's grace. We commend everything to Him. Lord, take care of Ruddy and the children of the ghetto.

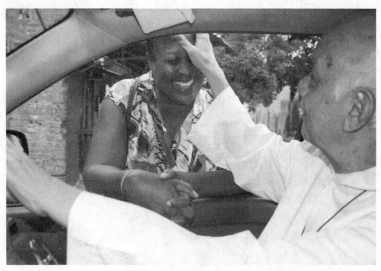

God bless you.

Chapter Thirty-Two

> *"Jesus bent down and wrote with his finger on the ground. And as they continued to ask him, he stood up and said to them, 'Let him who is without sin among you be the first to throw a stone at her.' And once more he bent down and wrote with his finger on the ground. But when they heard it, they went away . . . and Jesus was left alone with the woman standing before him. Jesus looked up and said to her, 'Woman, where are they? Has no one condemned you?' She said, 'No one, Lord.' And Jesus said, 'Neither do I condemn you.'"*
>
> Jn 8:6b-11a

SHE lived near Kingston Public Hospital and made merry with men in a bar where she was a bar maid. A witty woman with a wide smile and a large booming laugh, Janet was a good companion for men who had gone to the bar in search of some form of escape or for great fun.

It cost her three children, which she did not regret. They were a blessing to her despite the dreadful burden of being hit-by-night siblings. The terrible tears and burden of guilt was relieved by a penitential life of motherhood which purified the inner pain and sense of degradation Janet suffered every night in the bar. She laughed all the more in her sadness so that men would take her with even greater lust and aggression. Being loved or rather being wanted, even though only sexually, gave Janet a sense of definition, purpose, a sense of being needed for something.

The three children were ashamed. Even in the kindergarten other children told them, "Your mother is a whore." They were perplexed and ashamed and later became violent. "Is not true, you hear," Janet told Stephen, her eldest. But the school kids kept teasing them even though Stephen had left a few eyes cut and a broken nose on two smaller boys and a little girl.

Then Janet ran away from her children and her job at the bar. She was ashamed for her little ones and left them to her sister. Every now and then she would send some money to Sibyl to take care of the children.

Janet continued her life of prostitution for two years as she wandered from home to home and slept sometimes in the street. Her body shrank, and she became weakened. Finally Janet went to KPH where she was given tests. Then the declaration was made: Janet had AIDS. She was petrified, mortified. "Oh my God, and my mother gave me education, she gave me food and clothes and send me to Sunday school. What happen? How this happen?" She turned inward as she recalled how her step-father had abused her sexually. When Janet told her mother, she refused to believe her, and Janet ran out of the house. That's the way she ended at St. George's Lane.

The Brothers were called to pick her up. Janet was lying near the hospital. She was so weak she could hardly move. Brother John and Brother Anil took her in.

Though 38 years old, Janet seemed well over 60 years. She was shrivelled thin like a fallen mango, green and dry without use or purpose. Her eyes were dead, and there seemed to be a fungus all over her body which whitened and dulled her black skin. She gazed vacantly at Brother John when he asked if she could sit up: in truth, she could do nothing for herself. But cared for, bathed, fed, given medications, she improved over the weeks. She wanted to help and would sweep the yard at our home. But the relentless virus would not be denied. She suffered excruciating head pain as her body succumbed to this hideous disease. Thank God the pain was replaced by coma and, at last, that deep sleep of death.

And praise God! She was reconciled with her children. The Brothers visited Sibyl and Janet's children and brought the children to their mother. They visited regularly, with great love and forgiveness. This brought great peace to Janet and made her dying easier.

Yes, those who are afflicted by AIDS are people. They are our Jamaican people. Christ is in them, and they are God's children. They might have sinned, and sinned greatly. They might have passed on AIDS to others. But we cannot be cruel, and we must not be self-righteous. Rather, we must show them God's love, mercy, and forgiveness. Let us remember and re-enact that great promise of the Lord in the time of Hosea when the people had committed harlotry by forsaking the Lord:

> "I will betroth you to me . . . in steadfast love, and in mercy. I will betroth you to me in faithfulness; and you shall know the Lord."

> Hos 2:19-20

Faith Centre. We have no home; we will trust in the Lord.

Chapter Thirty-Three

....

"We . . . are being changed into his likeness.
We have renounced disgraceful, underhanded ways."

2 Cor 3:18a; 4:2a

RAYMOND is getting married! Once a thieving ghetto man, now a Christian. I am not talking about a sudden "Hallelujah!" This man swallowed the word of God four years ago. It was planted in good soil and has been brought to fruition by the kiss of God's love. Now Raymond has matured into full adulthood; now he is in his full flowering.

He used to come around Faith Centre. He was then twenty-four, and he had not worked for six years. Once he was a thief, but he was shocked to his senses after six months in a severe prison. When he came out, he discovered his baby mother had another child. That made two, and she had disappeared.

He volunteered at Faith Centre: "I'll do anything. I don't want to sit around. Just give me a lunch, Father." He picked up paper, swept the yard, worked in the garden. Then he would eat lunch and leave reluctantly for he wanted to stay around longer. "I don't want no more negativity. I prefer to do something with myself, anything, even for nothing."

He got a promotion: he started working in the kitchen and stores. We gave him a package of groceries and a little money each week. Then he said a few of his friends asked if they could make shoes using our premises. They would need a little space and some help in organization. Raymond did well. Quietly and persistently he worked through discouragement and fights

135

with co-workers. Then suddenly the project closed: the company wanted no more shoes. We gave him a job as a manual labourer. Again he worked steadily without a word of complaint, but only a daily smile and a prayer of thanksgiving.

One day I caught him with some small cast-away building materials—old wood and nails. I was very severe with him, not because of the goods, but he hadn't asked permission. And I knew he had a sensitive conscience, something I didn't want him to lose. I suspended him for a week. After he came back, he showed his ability to work through tiredness, disappointment, and pressure from the other ghetto men. He had in him a sense of determination which grew out of a serious commitment to being a man and a provider for his two children.

Raymond sat beside me in the garden. It was noon time, and he had worked all morning. I was moved with a great love for him. How could this man who suffered all the diabolic evils of ghetto life be so true, so good? He was born into poverty and violence. His mother had been abandoned by her baby father with the children. He suffered from semi-literacy, joblessness, hunger, and even prison. Yet here he sat beside me, a compact man, full of goodness and self-respect, without a trace of arrogance or machismo.

His arms were wet in the faded blue ganzie. He pulled off his cap and wiped his brow. For a few minutes there was silence between us; then we looked at each other and smiled and laughed. We shook hands, then hugged each other. Back to silence. Then the man-to-man talk began.

"Father, is it right for me to marry Helen? Or she must have a baby by me first?"

I laughed. Well, if this wasn't Jamaican culture at the roots! I assured him that the Church would really be glad that he wouldn't have any children until after the marriage. He smiled broadly. "Anything you say, Father."

"Can you take care of her, Raymond, and the little pickney girl she has from her first baby father?"

"Yes, Father. God gave me strength to work. I can do it."

"What date do you want to set for the wedding?"

"As soon as can be," he hastily replied.

Raymond has come to church every Sunday. He is always on time. He doesn't smoke, drink, gamble, nor take on women. Once he did, but not again. "I like to keep by myself and the children. I happy now. When I was wild, I thought I was happy. I was merry, but not happy. Now I don't have confusion. Now I have peace of mind.

"The little dollars I get, I come to stretch it. You learn when you have to, with the two little pickney. And the wood the Brothers give me—look at the nice house I have now. I never thought I would see the day."

Raymond is not only a man who had come to help himself. He begged a piece of land for an old lady—Myrtle and her children—and he himself spent hours after work and on weekends and built her a two-room house without charge.

Raymond is a miracle of God's love. God has moulded him, making him more and more into His image and likeness. Someday—maybe—others will follow his footsteps, and ghetto men will become husbands and fathers, capable and stable enough to undertake long-term commitments and responsibilities. And maybe, even further, they will care for other poor brothers and sisters in the ghetto. It can be done with the power of God's grace.

We have fifty homes—monasteries, residences for the homeless—in thirteen diocese among the poorest. Only you and God will provide for His people.

Chapter Thirty-Four

"For thou hast been a stronghold to the poor,
a stronghold to the needy in his distress,
a shelter from the storm."

Is 25:4

OUR gate was flung open as if by the hands of a mighty giant. It jammed, and we could not close it back; each time we tried, Hurricane Gilbert flung us back. Outside our gate the ghetto youths were roaming the streets in packs, charged with excitement, breaking into stores, looting and running with packages. Occasionally, we heard a series of gunshots, shouting, and screaming, but there was also much laughing.

The wildness of the hurricane was bacchanal, arousing turbulent emotions. Lawlessness and carousing seemed to take control of the blood of the ghetto youth. People danced in the rain and the wind with wild abandon. They enjoyed the danger of the menacing hurricane and seemed to dare it. This dangerous mood pervaded the ghetto during the storm. I found it strange and disturbing, no less so than the mood of Hurricane Gilbert itself.

Practically speaking, I also feared that Faith Centre would be invaded by gunmen. That mob psychology, looting, and shooting might be brought through our iron gate thrown back by the storm. During those most terrifying twenty-four hours from midnight Sunday to midnight Monday, that gate was like the open mouth of a river. But no gunman, no thief came in, only the old, the blind, the crippled, the helpless came. Some were

139

lifted up bodily by young people in the slums; some walked on the arms of others.

The Brothers stayed round-the-clock at Jacob's Well and Faith Centre during the hurricane week. Except for brief sleep they never stopped working. Such generosity! Together with people of the ghetto who work and volunteer all year long, the Brothers dealt solemnly but effectively with the mothers, their children, old folks, and all types of people who were struck severely by Hurricane Gilbert.

Person after person came in. Crowds of people were stuffed onto bed after improvised bed. People who cannot read and write became alive with intelligence, running in and out of Faith Centre, lifting in the middle of Gilbert's most dreadful moments of anger, people blind, old, feeble, crippled, rescuing their lives from death and total disaster. Food, cocoa, biscuits were organized into the hands of our refugees. Here and there candles were lit, and prayers were said.

Fifteen women packed up food and cooked and never stopped. Pearl, head of them all, kept the pot boiling for seventy-two hours until I ordered her home. The Brothers moved out into the ghettoes and climbed roofs. I don't know how many people's lives touched ours that week. I only know that God moved through the hearts of our Brothers, our workers, and volunteers. Each one worked with a driving grace that could only have come from God alone.

I give thanks and praise for the generosity and for our safety. But also none of our buildings at any of our sites was damaged seriously. It was as if only the hair of our head was ruffled, and it could easily be brushed back.

There are disasters, however. Sleeping at the Faith Centre was like sleeping on a storm-tossed ship, but although there were periods of real terror, we were safe. Others have not survived the calamity. A breadfruit tree was ripped out of the ground; it killed Lenora, granny of one of our workers. The whole shack was smashed. Another tree—a giant mango—was split as if by an axe held by the mighty hand of God. It fell on five more shacks, three on the right, two on the left.

Hurricane Gilbert bore a lash in its hand: relentlessly it whipped the ghettoes. In central Kingston, just about everybody lost and found zinc. Zinc sheets were lifted like birds aloft by the wind. Thousands and thousands of people are in broken-down shacks, beaten down by wind and rain. There are old and young men and women, mothers and their children without roofs on their miserable little rooms, miserable before with tattered zinc now broken or gone, wood patched with torn plastic now broken and shredded. And everything is wet: clothes are soaked; mattresses are moist or soaked; floors are all mud. Each night, people are sleeping in their hovels. They were not blessed with safe buildings as we were. They sleep under the sky; they sleep in their shacks in order to protect the little they have left. They know there was looting; they know their own poor will prey upon them.

There is no water, there is no light, and the streets are packed with dead limbs of trees and telephone and power poles. Garbage is piled up over the walls. People who lived through the storm now worry how they are going to live today and tomorrow. How will they send the children back to school? Their houses are mashed up, there is no money. Their lives are in confusion.

We must now bend our backs to the task: the Cross. We must quickly wipe away the tears. All of us: nailing, rebuilding, washing, cleaning. The spirit must prevail. We must carry the Cross with strength from Calvary to Mount Zion.

A handcart can help me make a living.

Chapter Thirty-Five

....

"He who closes his ear to the cry of the poor will himself cry out and not be heard."

Prov 21:13

HURRICANE Gilbert bulldozed hundreds of thousands of poor Jamaicans. I don't know how the relief will get to those who are homeless, and by this time, forty days later, there are many for whom the hurricane is a direct road to the madhouse.

Ronald Henry came to me, "Father, I have been walking on the road ever since the hurricane. My house blew down. It wasn't mine, and the landlord said I had to leave; he needed the space now. So I left the one room with Marcia, my wife, and the three children."

I looked at the baby. It was fast asleep in his arms, but it was thin and discoloured, grey rather than black in colour. Marcia stood in the background, her face drawn and thin; and two little kiddies, a little boy and girl, stood by her sucking their fingers, and with big hungry eyes and skinny little limbs.

"I've slept on the roadside and under bus sheds for six weeks. I'm going off my head, Father. If it was I alone, I wouldn't worry. But my wife and little children."

It was a situation that made me feel helpless and somewhat confused. Kingston is so overcrowded and lacking in dwellings. What could I tell this good man? He is devoted to his wife and children and has a job. In days past, people would have taken him in, somehow. They would have squeezed him in. But the ghetto yards are piled up, shack upon shack, with men, with mothers and children, and next door, aunties and uncles and other distant relatives. No one can find a room in the ghetto; there is no space in the yard to build yet another shack, but the people keep piling in.

"Ronald, why don't you go to the country?"

"No one there, Father."

"No relatives in Kingston?"

"No, Father."

"None of your wife's relatives are around?"

"No space, Father."

I called the family together and looked at their faces. They were solemn and speechless. It was as if they were defeated: no smiles, no life, no hope. It was disturbing. They seemed like the Holy Family—Jesus, Mary, and Joseph—and there was no room in the inn.

"I have no room here, not even temporary shelter, Ronald."

"Where can we go?"

There was nothing practical I could do. This vexed me. I could only try to turn their minds to the star of Bethlehem. "Keep looking. You must find a place. If you don't, come back and at least put your head down on the floor of our chapel."

We gave them a little soup. I blessed them, and they went. "Remember, come back if you must. Don't sleep on the sidewalk with the children."

They did not come back. Bur their haggard and defeated faces come back to me. Where are they now? Will they just add to the number of street people we see throughout Kingston? Will they go mad? Will the children stray like dogs on the street? The numbers of our homeless will increase, not due to Hurricane Gilbert alone, but because we have not heard the cry of the poor. They need to be attended to; they are like children without parents, lost in the wilderness of a mixed-up and confused society. If their hearts stop beating and our eyes are dry, without tears, our hearts will also stop beating. We will still be breathing, but love will have died and so will we.

Oh Lord, in you I trust. Never let me be afraid.

Chapter Thirty-Six

·······························

"Blessed be the God and Father of our Lord Jesus
Christ, the Father of mercies and God of all comfort,
who comforts us in all our affliction."

2 Cor 1:3-4a

COMPTON died of AIDS. Rebecca heard his body shiver and then he stretched out stiffly with a long last breath and his hand fell over the bedside. From her sleep Rebecca suddenly shrieked and leapt from the crocus bags which were her bed. It was two o'clock in the morning. The moonlight seemed like the light of God through the window; she saw that Compton's eyes were wide open. Kissing his mouth, she then closed it and whispered, "May you rest in peace."

It was two full weeks she hadn't left his bedside. Anything he needed, she sent the little children for. Rebecca gave him crackers or box juice; at the end he rejected the little cooked foods she was able to provide. "You have to fatten up if you want to live," she told Compton. But the dark stranger had taken hold of him and would not leave until Compton was ready for pilgrimage to the afterworld.

Day by day his cheeks had become more hollow as if the dark stranger was hewing away a giant tree with a cutlass. At the end, the bones in his face were sharp like a knife. And little flies pitched around his lips and nostrils, predatory birds awaiting their fill. But the grim reaper was not to outdo Rebecca: the more love she gave, the more her love intensified. She hardly wept a tear. She bathed him often as he sweated: his hands, his forehead, and his entire body. And she sang, as Jamaican women do in the depths of their sorrow, "Mother, at your feet is kneeling, one who loves you, this your child." Compton became pale and yellow, that she could not help; but the bristles of hair on his chin had no chance to make unkempt his appearance: Rebecca shaved him and dried his face daily.

With a mother's eye and a mother's love, Rebecca found him beautiful. There was no anger in her for having to attend to him all these days and nights. Every other activity she stopped; she wanted to do nothing else even though she herself would perhaps lose the job she had as a washer woman in Vineyard Town. She stayed with him quietly and purposefully as if she was fulfilling the complete meaning of her life. Nothing else mattered; everything else was secondary. Until death would she part. Rebecca told me that he was beautiful, and she felt that on his deathbed he was like her first baby.

When they were in the graveyard, Pam, the one solitary visitor at the funeral, had to steady Rebecca by the grave. Pam had to hold her firmly around the shoulders as Rebecca choked back the tears. The little boy and girl looked on solemnly, Patrick in his little black bow tie and Pansy in her dress with bows in her hair. "Compton has gone back to the Father. He has been taken from you, and he has passed these two little ones for you, Rebecca, to care for," Fr. Arthur counselled.

Rebecca heard these words as if the divine will had been given to her by Father Arthur, who presided over the burial service, and she did not let another tear fall. She turned to the two little ones and placed a hand around Patrick and Pansy. After she had thrown a little dirt on the coffin, she walked away. She knew she had another purpose; the words of Jesus at the foot of the Cross came back to her: "Woman, behold thy son. Son, behold thy mother." The job was not finished; there were still her grandchildren.

Chapter Thirty-Seven

....

"It is easier for a camel to go through the eye of a needle than for a rich man to enter the kingdom of heaven."

Mt 19:24

A IR Jamaica said, "Yes." They want to help us with our projects for the poor. American Airlines is also a tremendous help. Our overseas concerts are a splendid source of revenue, not to mention the wonderful fellowship among the singers, musicians, audiences, and organizers. Nobody gets any pay, nobody wants any pay: all goes to the poor and to no one else. Air Jamaica had no hesitation: all three overseas journeys would be paid for. They know that our poor are in need. Air Jamaica even sent a nurse, once weekly, to minister to our sick. Food, clothes, and an assortment of goods abandoned at the airport come our way.

We have other generous benefactors who are prominent in the business community. I do not condemn businessmen or their opinions. I do condemn selfishness, however; and I do encounter selfishness among the rich. I meet selfishness in the poor as well, but the selfish poor are not in a position to help. The wealthy businessmen are the power in the island.

I also believe too few businessmen promote the stability of this island over their own pursuit of millions. Businessmen are needed, badly needed, but they must be men with ambiance and vision who see business in the context of the overall good of the nation. While attending to their own companies, they must also pursue justice for the more than a million of our people who are poor. Such businessmen understand that stability requires a greater equity among our people. This can only be obtained by an outpouring of love, a huge sense of self-sacrifice—businessmen working as businessmen, building up their businesses, but giving substantially, not crumbs of their table, and initiating businesses that are less in profit, but authentic and lasting, rooted in our own land, drawn from our resources, within the capacity of our poor undereducated and underemployed people.

There is the beginning of kindness in our island, but only the beginning. There is also extensive and substantial selfishness. What do I mean by substantial selfishness?

"Can you come and bless my house. Father?"

"We can squeeze it in. How is the business?"

"Things are not what they should be, and the workers won't work."

"I need a couple of bags of cornmeal."

There is hesitation. Then, "Things are very tight, but we can manage."

I was picked up in a Rolls Royce. I understand that a Rolls Royce, if importation is allowed, costs one-and-a-half million Jamaican dollars; that is nearly forty thousand U.S. dollars. An entire family of five in the ghetto with the mother fully employed have to live on one hundred and twenty-five dollars a week or about four U.S. dollars. Two bags of cornmeal, five people's lives over and against the cost of a vehicle!

Is this our island's value system? Certainly it is to this Christian gentleman. A further question: how can we have stability in our island in a situation like this? Isn't this part of why the poor man is running down the drug trade? As I observe it, there is a shocking amount of opulent vehicles that belong to millionaires' row in an island where most of our people are poor.

When I went to the goodly gentleman's house, a favour I did because he had been a school-mate of mine and a Catholic, I was shocked. The house was built on the side of hill: three stories high, twenty-four rooms. It reminded me of a Chinese pagoda. Red ceiling tiles contrasted with the pure white of the rest of the house. The entire building, my host stated, was imported from the Far East: fine bone china, ivory, burnished gold, and brass. The tables and chairs were moulded by hand, lacquered and carved in gold and black. Delicate carvings and vases, silk flowers, artificial but beautifully shaped, were placed in the drawing and dining rooms, screened with silken drapes. The yard simulated an oriental garden: plants shaped along horizontal lines, goldfish ponds, rocks, peacocks. A Chinese emperor's home.

There was hesitation when I had asked for two bags of cornmeal for the poor. "Things are not what they should be."

Young Brothers at prayer. Prayer is the only answer.

Chapter Thirty-Eight

....

"But when he heard this he became sad, for he was
very rich."

Lk 18:23

"NO, I don't intend to have my son waste his time. Carl is to go down to Trinidad and become an engineer like his father. After his education, we don't intend to waste him on being a priest or brother. I am asking you, Fr. Ho Lung, to discontinue your contact with him."

"You don't want your boy to serve God? The boy wants God and to serve the people."

"Church is enough. I don't want him becoming a fanatic—especially this business about the poor. You can't build a house with that or feed or clothe yourself."

"God, through the Church, will provide these things for him."

"I don't think you understand. I don't want you to interfere with him. He is my child. He is none of your business."

Carl is nineteen. His mother is Catholic, but she doesn't follow Christ. She only goes to church.

"Why send him to a Catholic school then?"

"To educate and discipline him."

"Priests and sisters sacrifice their whole lives to serve your children and people like yourself."

"That's their business."

Carl came to me confused. His mother had told him charity work is for when you have time. "We must be practical, Father. My mother is right. I must get these things done first;

otherwise I'll never be happy. Then maybe later on, I could do a little thing."

Charity, it seems, is perceived as crumbs off the master's table. Yet Jesus tells us that we must seek first the kingdom of God and everything else will follow. The one norm he gives in judging whether we are designated for hell or heaven is our love for the poor. "Feed the hungry, clothe the naked, welcome the stranger. . . . If you do it to the least of my brethren, you do it unto me." I told all this to Carl, but he shook his head and went away.

What is education today? People seek it as an opportunity to move away from the poor to the middle class and from the middle to the upper class. Modern economics and business have contrived it that family life, work, politics, and especially education be trapped behind the high prison walls of mammon. If one is to survive, money, plain and simple, lots of it, is required to obtain a simple necessity such as a house. The training of the intellect, without interference from the emotions, is what gives us the power to control and contrive ways of becoming rich.

And what of the schooling of the heart? The humanities which arouse and inform our sense of pity and love have been abrogated to that one intention, to build up personal security. We must make it financially. All other concerns, such as other people's survival, must not be diluted by inconvenient emotions which take us away from that singular purpose: to make money. Thus, in a strange irony, education abstracts us from reality: the destitution, loneliness, and manner of death which most of our fellow men suffer. Today the humanizing which the arts are meant to accomplish is labelled useless.

No matter how rich, no matter how brilliant we are, however, once the heart stops beating, a man is dead. Love is what stirs the heart and keeps a man alive. But for those who care only for their own, for those who espouse to that most unchristian of beliefs—that charity begins at home—they will never know the fear and enthrallment of complete abandonment and the absolute excitement of loving and being loved by God and His little people.

I believe our humanity is finally tested by our ability to love, by the greatness of our hearts. The more we can love, the more people we can serve with joy—especially the grotesque and the outcast—the more human we become. We cannot fathom the terror and the beauty when we love absolutely, without condition, all God's children. My prayer for the Brothers and myself is, "Would that we would love more." And that others would partake of our happiness by serving the least of our brethren.

But Carl could not believe in that kind of happiness. He could not give up all he had to follow Christ. And so the rich young man went away sad.

Do you love me? Feed my lamb, feed my sheep.

Chapter Thirty-Nine

....

"Jesus said, 'Take away the stone.' Martha, the sister of the dead man, said to him, 'Lord, by this time there will be an odour, for he has been dead four days.' Jesus said to her, 'Did I not tell you that if you would believe you would see the glory of God?'"

Jn 11:39-40

I alternated between anger and sadness. There has never been a more revolting human sight or smell. We don't know his name, but we call him Lazarus because he was in the tomb.

A telephone call came from a gentleman. "He is going to die. I don't know what to do. He has been on Peter's Lane for the last three weeks. Do you pick up?" Brother Ambrose replied that we don't since we have trouble with transport. "Brother, he is going to die."

Brother Ambrose called Faith Centre. Our driver had just driven in. Brother Max dashed down to Peter's Lane behind General Post Office. A crowd had gathered in a large circle. The smell of putrefied flesh turned the stomach of anyone within forty feet. People gazed at him at a distance as if on a spectre. He was like so many of the walking dead we see around the city: black with soot, meagre to the skin, and bedraggled, a head like a black dyed mop turned upside down and caked with mud.

Brother Max startled everyone by rushing past the crowd and scooping him in his arms despite the smell of rotten flesh and the horde of flies. Lazarus curled up in our van just as we had found him, as though he was in his mother's womb:

both hands crossing his chest, eyes closed as in deep sleep, and knees bent to his waist.

At Faith Centre, Sister Mary Rose came forward. Looking at the big wound on his head was like looking into the pit of hell. Maggots, hundreds of maggots squirmed on his head. All the flesh had been eaten away except for the outer circle of hair which edged and dropped in lengthy locks. Only because our brothers and sisters have had to attend to so many wounds and sores at our centres did no one vomit. But the smell was stale, dead flesh, like a dead rat. And no one will forget the sight of the maggots wriggling in the flesh and discoloured blood on the crown of his head.

All were stunned into silence. Yet everyone knew what to do. Brother Louima took off Lazarus' rags and began bathing away the layer of mud on his body. He did so calmly, silently. Then he washed Lazarus' face and shaved and cut back the drooping locks. The sisters got him pants, a shirt, underwear. Brother Max went for hydrogen peroxide and forced Lazarus to sit up. Then he poured it on the writhing maggots.

The sisters and brothers began to remove the maggots one by one with long medical forceps. Because the maggots had set in for so long, they were deep in the flesh, where there was flesh. For four long hours, they picked away at the maggots. All this time, there was silence, and Lazarus sat with eyes closed as if in a deep sleep. Wound powder was applied with the hope of destroying all those devilish white worms in his skull, most of which could now be seen. All the dead flesh that could be removed was cut away patiently. At last, there emerged his gleaming white skull, like a crown of glory.

Christ moved in the hearts of our religious brothers and sisters as they worked away with the broken body of this poor man. They felt in themselves an increase of love and compassion.

Every moment, every second was warm as new life passed into their blood and into their hearts as they attended the sacred body of Lazarus, the least of our brothers. They were calm and prayerful, and a mysterious event overtook them, something that cannot be comprehended or spoken in words: it was the infusion of God's grace, which came from Lazarus into them; it was the presence of God that they were encountering in this man. God entered them without them being conscious of it. It was no less real but equally as invisible as the heat of the sun which penetrates the earth and makes it warm and full of life, filling everything in our material world—beasts of the air and sea and even the dead and inert mud from which we are made—with life.

When the brothers and sisters had completed their work, they were gay as the hint of a smile passed his lips after being asked, "Are you feeling better?" Was it not the body of Christ taken down from the Cross that they attended to? In Lazarus, was it not the sacred image of Christ they had seen, in the likeness of whom everyone of us has been made? Wasn't Lazarus an existential experience of God's outpouring of grace and consolation in the hearts of his sons and daughters, a reward given for doing Christ's work?

Lazarus is now at Faith Centre. Last evening the Brothers reflected and prayed over the coming of Lazarus to our home: Christ in the disguise of the poor. Brother Max and the others meditated on the terror of the sight and the smell, the repulsiveness of the work, the sadness of his suffering, and yet the deep encounter with Christ, the experience of fulfilment, and the love of their vocations and the crucified Lord they had experienced that day.

I feel sad that there is so much disregard and cold-heartedness in our island. Hundreds walked by Lazarus on Peter's Lane in the heart of our city, and for three weeks no one took responsibility for him, a poor man who is our brother in Christ, until that one call came. I feel angry at the malicious devil who struck Lazarus on the head and left him wounded on the street: he must be punished.

But I also feel joy, the joy of experiencing and doing Christ's work. Nothing, absolutely nothing else can bring the experience of happiness the brothers and sisters had in attending to Lazarus, who is now risen from the dead. Jesus said, "Lazarus, come out," and "Unbind him, and let him go." Not only Lazarus, but all of us had been set free in the encounter of that day.

Chapter Forty

....

> *"Neither death, nor life, nor angels, nor princi-*
> *palities, nor things present, nor things to come, nor*
> *powers, nor height, nor depth, nor anything else in*
> *all creation, will be able to separate us from the love*
> *of God in Christ Jesus our Lord."*
>
> Rom 8:38-39

I remember a very stark image in southern India. I visited there in order to interview some young men who had applied to join the Brothers. I saw there an immense and vast poverty that I had never before imagined or seen.

There are 900 million people in that nation. The people are as plentiful as the dust of the dry parched land. There is little water, little food. But the people take care of everything; nothing is thrown out. Everything is carefully used: paper is recycled, drain water is caught and reused. The cold floor and sidewalks, rather than mattresses, are used for sleeping. Every object is a precious gift from God. Most important: every person, no matter how poor, is well regarded.

I saw a man, his wife, and their child under a make-shift shed, worked with dry coconut leaves. The baby appeared to be dying of hunger. The father and mother were skin and bones. They too were half on their journey to dust. They were in each other's arms, the baby between them sucking at the dry breast of the mother. It was an image at the same time gruesome and beautiful: an entire family dying of hunger in each other's arms. There was no weeping, no shouts of anger, only silence in the hot sun. People passed by without shock or laughter, as though it were commonplace—a strange peace as death cradled them in his arms.

These people are materially poor, much poorer than the poor of Jamaica; but they are spiritually rich, wealthier than materially rich families who are not spawned in love and not given care. Husbands, wives, and children need to be in each other's arms, giving one another to each other, rather than giving things as a substitute for their presence to each other. We are meant to be a holy family like Joseph, Mary, and Jesus: brought up in love with a deep and profound respect for God and for one another.

"But I provide everything for my wife, even thing for my children—home, school, clothes, food, and more. Why are we unhappy?"

We cannot buy off one another with goods, nor can we exchange pleasure for love. Being with one another, spending time with our loved ones, working together, teaching one another, suffering together, praying together: this is what love is. Presence to one another and a prayerful recognition of God, of His will, of what is right, and of what is wrong—all these are the essential components of love. Television, entertainment, new clothes, a new home, travel—all these are ashes unless there be presence to one another. To me, culture is care, the habits of the heart, the habits of justice and mercy and self-control. Culture is more than the masterpieces of great paintings and sculpture. Culture is a living thing: people living in harmony, gently loving one another, and consciously aware of one another as a divine mystery, with God within, precious as gold to the Creator and to others.

That poor Indian family taught me that neither short nor long life, neither poverty nor riches can take away love. This is a people who have not plenty. Yet the Hindu religion has made them spiritually rich, reverential to nature and to man, bound together in family life, and most respectful to God Himself. No doubt there is abuse and sin, but the system of belief, the stress on God and the supernatural, the respect for authority and law: these are in place, and so there is much peace and harmony in this most ancient of cultures. Well might we learn from them how to build community, selflessness, and holy families.

I am my brothers keeper.

Chapter Forty-One

....

"And they rose that same hour, and returned to Jerusalem; and they found the eleven gathered together and those who were with them. Then they told what had happened on the road, and how he was known to them in the breaking of the bread."

Lk 24:33, 35

ANGELLA sits on the floor. Her arms are grotesquely contorted, fixed rigidly behind her back. They have no functional use. Nor can she walk. Someone has to bathe her, dress her, comb her hair, brush her teeth, wipe her bottom. Feeding is a major challenge, for her head jerks spastically and uncontrollably. She emits strangled sounds which—if you listen carefully—resemble words.

People will say, "How sad!" "Pathetic." "It would be better if she had died at birth."

But they have not seen her face, nor looked into her eyes. When she sees a friend, she swings her body around, and her mouth bursts into a full, broad smile. Her teeth gleam. Her eyes sparkle and dance. All that she is is focused in her face: she is love, pure incarnate love, the word made flesh!

No, she is neither sad nor pathetic. She is vibrantly alive, and she is beautiful.

People sometimes ask why we do what we do. Why do we work with the poor? What do we accomplish? Aren't there more important, more relevant things to do? Don't we get discouraged by the vast world of human suffering, by the evils of slum life?

What can I say! I look into Angella's face and see Jesus! And what is more, if Jesus is the mediator between me and all my experience, then I am not decreased but increased by my works with the poor. I meet Christ in them more and more. And when one is stretched out and gives to the poor all that one is and all that one has, the eloquence of that moves people to love one another. With the eyes of faith, if Jesus is alive in us, this is language that can be understood and which lasts forever.

Love. It is like lighting a candle in the darkness. When we love the poor, we and they become alive. The heart pounds; the mind burns. Yes, I know that many of the poor are not considered to be productive members of society. How, after all, does one develop and empower Angella or Miriam, who is severely retarded, or Kenneth, who is mad, or Mr. Morgan, who is senile, or Miss June, who is dying? Their production consists in this, that they love and care for one another: one person bathing another, one person cleaning another's mess, a little deaf and dumb boy leading an old blind woman, Frankie washing the men's clothing, Everel mopping the floor. Countless small acts constituting great love.

The poor are Christ. Being with the poor is a little thing, but this little thing stirs a flame of love and what remains for the poor is not the work, nor anything given, not food, nor clothes, but that we were together, physically together. Being with the poor is absorbed into the life of the living God of love and our smallest acts are transformed into life that is eternal and that has unlimited value. This is the sustaining vision which brings power and joy and real transformation of one's work with the poor.

A little given to all, a little fish, a little bread, common things become the body and blood of Christ. Luke's story of the two disciples on the road to Emmaus after Christ's crucifixion is palpable to us because of the poor. Seated with the disciples at supper, Jesus took the bread, broke it, and gave it to them: "With that their eyes were opened and they recognized him."

We have sunshine in the ghettos—no need for washing machines.

Chapter Forty-Two

....

"And God said, 'This is the sign of the covenant
which I make between me and you and every living
creature that is with you, for all future generations: I
set my bow in the cloud, and it shall be a sign of the
covenant between me and the earth.'"

Gen 9:12-13

DESMOND'S arm, no shorter than a broom stick, reached through the louvres and picked up the two blackie mangoes on my plate. I was startled. Then off he bounded with a big grin across his face. Everybody laughed. Desmond, who nobody thought was capable of doing anything: he doesn't think, he doesn't feel, he doesn't communicate whether by language or by sign. Just a human person born into the world to be and for us to love him just as he is.

One Sunday, Father Hayden and I were saying Mass at Faith Centre. Two hundred people were at the Mass. The altar boys were beautifully bedecked in white robes and green sashes. The choir had rung out songs of praise and jubilation. I had preached this most serious sermon about the Cross, and everyone had acknowledged my points with a head shake. Then came the most serious part of the Mass: the solemn consecration of the bread and wine into the body and blood of Christ. Father Hayden lifted the bread; the bells rang: "This is my body."

As if from out of nowhere, in ran Desmond, stark naked before the altar, with his clothes neatly compiled in his hands. His long arms and legs made him look like a kangaroo. One of our other residents chased after him and quickly ushered him to the dormitory. We couldn't subdue our laughter. If that wasn't a moment only that master of humour, God Himself, could have planned!

Desmond is untrained, and every now and then does something socially awkward. Yesterday, he chose my fish pond to sit by and rock back and forth. When he wanted to pee, he simply turned sideways, pulled out his teapot and peed right into the fish pond. My poor gold fish must have been shocked by the assault of a strange new substance. A few may have given up the ghost. Desmond rolled over and continued to bask in the sun.

This strange creature is a source of wonderment to everyone at Faith Centre. He is abnormally tall and skinny but for a bloated belly. His colour is jet black, and his teeth, separate and chalk white, fly out of his mouth in a gruesome manner. I remember Wayne and Desmond having a collision when Desmond first came to Faith Centre. Desmond had a deep and wide cut and was bleeding profusely, but he registered no pain. Even feelings of great pain are dead to him.

Desmond is autistic. Poor Relief brought him here. He was terrified of people. Anytime someone drew near, he covered his head with his hands as if he was going to be struck. Most of the time, he still sits by himself by the garden and rocks back and forth. He escapes into his own world, absorbed in imaginative activity which bars him from the experience of his surroundings.

But he is here now. Little did we know when we took him that he would become valuable to us. What delight it is to see growth in these forgotten ones. Sonia, one of our workers, chases him around the grounds and tickles him. Desmond laughs uproariously. Wayne helps to dress him and takes him to prayer. Pearl sits down and makes sign language to him. Desmond loves it all.

Today we measure human life according to its productivity. If only we could understand the beauty and value of life for itself and in itself. Desmond is indeed a jewel, but we cannot measure him in terms of dollars and cents. He is just meant to be, and for us it is a matter of being filled with wonder and awe at God's rainbow-world, so different, so interesting. There is laughter also, at the foot of the Cross, once we see the world through the eyes of the Maker Himself.

Brothers to one another and brothers of the poor.

Chapter Forty-Three

"The Lord has risen indeed!"

Lk 24:34

OUR chapel was packed. Youths from the streets as well as old folks, little pickneys, school boys, mothers and grannies: all came wreathed in smiles. Mostly in white, the children nevertheless had the fanciest of hairdos bunched in a hundred groupings on top of their heads, with decorative rings around them or braided and intertwined with colourful ribbons. Old ladies and their teenage daughters had on their plain dresses, all starched and ironed, and on their hands were handbags and bangles. Smiles and more smiles were the best of all their decorations, however. They wanted to greet each other as well as their Lord and Saviour on this grand Easter mom.

Some folks from the ghetto had come and scrubbed our chapel floor in the old style red ochre and coconut brush. It was shining so you could almost see the reflection of your shoes and legs. There wasn't any cobweb in sight, and the wooden logs of our chapel walls had not a speck of dirt between the crevices.

Mass began incongruously with everyone singing "All the Way to Calvary." I had to stop the spontaneous singing amidst everyone's consternation and indignation. But they smiled when I pointed out that it was not Good Friday but Easter Sunday. Then they really got into "He Arose!" Jamaican style and sang or rather shouted their hearts out.

The retarded and Down's syndrome residents—actually most of our homeless—have an amazing sense of the Lord and the spiritual life. They keep silence when it is appropriate; they listen attentively when the sermon is being preached; they shout in approval when the preacher makes a good point. They sing the words of some of the songs and say some of the parts of the Mass. They kneel and bow their heads at the appropriate times. They acknowledge the word of God with "Alleluia!" and "Amen!" at the right times. At the consecration they are in a state of deep reverence just like anyone else in our chapel. I have even seen tears and states of ecstasy in our retarded. They remain still, very quiet and seem to descend to the depths of their being in a deep encounter with Christ or the Spirit. Prayer, worship, meditation palpably take place, and they unite with the Lord.

Christ tells us, "Suffer the little ones to come unto me," and indeed, we have witnessed Christ welcoming these, the least of our brothers and sisters, in a deep spiritual relationship in and outside times of worship. Truly God loves those who are humble and poor, and He gives to them the gift of Himself, which they in turn gratefully receive.

At the "Our Father," all hold hands: the crippled, the sick, the old, and the young women, the young men, and the little children. I closed my eyes and allowed myself to experience the joy of us all being children of God, and took in the promise of the Resurrection.

At the handshake of peace, our congregation—all poor people—thunderously clapped and sang and greeted one another with love and elation. It is a sight to see and an experience that is one and at the same time spirit-filled as well as social. Our poor are really a family even amidst the squabbles and overcrowding and destitution. Somehow God is among them; somehow He is present among these broken-hearted people in a special way.

Yes, the work is tough. There is suffering and death and ugliness and endless struggle, but at the foot of the Cross, there is also the joy and happiness and the experience of Christ, not only the crucified Christ, but the One who is to come, the risen Christ, and the everlasting happiness he has promised us in his heavenly kingdom.

For donations and queries check the following:

MOP Website: www.missionariesofthepoor.org

MISSIONARIES OF THE POOR, USA
P.O. Box 29893, Atlanta GA 30359
(404)-248-1197
E-mail: mopusaoffice@missionariesofthepoor.org
Contact Person: Jane Rodgers, MOP Asso.

MISSIONARIES OF THE POOR, JAMAICA
P.O. Box 8525
3 North Street, Kingston C.S.O.
(876)-948-0280/(876)-967-0341
E-mail: mopja@missionariesofthepoor.org
Contact Person: Bro. Praful Barla, MOP.

MISSIONARIES OF THE POOR, CANADA
P.O. Box 20070 Southbrook PO
Maple, Ontario L6A 4K0, Canada
(905)-940-2606
E-mail: mopcanada@gmail.com
Contact person: Sera Rossi, MOP Asso.

GLOSSARY

a fe we God: God belongs to us
a so it go: that's the way it goes
baby father: father of her child
baby mother: mother of his child
Bellevue: mental hospital in Kingston
blackie mango: small, slightly astringent mango fruit
bruk: broke
buck-up: met
bulla cake: a cake of flour and molasses
callaloo: a leafy green edible garden vegetable similar to Swiss
    chard
cast: crossed
chile: child
chimmey: chamber pot
chiney: Chinese person
cho: exclamation showing impatience, scepticism, mild scorn,
    or the like
cho-cho: chayote: edible pear-shaped fruit of a vine of the
    cucumber family
coco: taro; edible tuberous root
Concrete Jungle: a Kingston ghetto
coolie: of East Indian origin
cotch: set or put; take temporary shelter or position
crocus bag: jute sack

dem: them

dey: is

dey bout: is there about

dis ya: this here

dust off: kill

Eventide: large public home for the poor, or almshouse, in Kingston

evilous: evil

Fadda! Me bredda come: Father, my brother has come (or my brother came)

fe: for or to

fe Him own pickney: God's own child

festival: oblong cake of cornmeal and flour fried in deep oil

fool-fool: foolish

foreign: abroad

ganja: marijuana

ganzie: T-shirt

going foreign: to go abroad

Gun Court: name commonly given to South Camp Rehabilitation Centre, a prison for men convicted of crimes involving guns

gwine: is going to; is happening

herbs: marijuana

higgler: street vendor

idren: soul brother

ina di: in the

is I a rule: I am the ruler

JDF: Jamaica Defence Force: the armed forces of Jamaica

JLP: Jamaica Labour Party, one of the two major political parties

john crow: turkey vulture

KPH: Kingston Public Hospital

lick: thrash

likkle: little
mash up: destroyed
me no know: I don't know
money dey bout: there is money there
nah: will not
nine night: the ninth night after the death when the spirit of the dead person is said to return before finally being consigned to the netherworld
nuh: now
pickney: child or children
PNP: People's National Party, one of the two major political parties
pon: upon
posse: gang that engages in criminal activities
rastaman: Rastafarian
second eleven: second team
so it go: that's the way it goes
spar: spar as in boxing, but in a friendly way
spliff: marijuana cigarette
suck-suck: coloured, flavoured ice confection
suck teeth: to make a disdainful sound with the teeth and mouth
tief: steal
vibes: intuition
we ina it: we are part of it
wid: with
yam: tropical climbing plant with edible starchy tuber

For donations and queries check the following:

MOP Website: www.missionariesofthepoor.org

MISSIONARIES OF THE POOR, USA
P.O. Box 29893, Atlanta GA 30359
(404)-248-1197
E-mail: mopusaoffice@missionariesofthepoor.org
Contact Person: Jane Rodgers, MOP Asso.

MISSIONARIES OF THE POOR, JAMAICA
P.O. Box 8525
3 North Street, Kingston C.S.O.
(876)-948-0280/(876)-967-0341
E-mail: mopja@missionariesofthepoor.org
Contact Person: Bro. Praful Barla, MOP.

MISSIONARIES OF THE POOR, CANADA
P.O. Box 20070 Southbrook PO
Maple, Ontario L6A 4K0, Canada
(905)-940-2606
E-mail: mopcanada@gmail.com
Contact person: Sera Rossi, MOP Asso.

ACKNOWLEDGMENTS

Grace Washington has been the primary person in giving form and shape to "Diary of a Ghetto Priest." I wrote these columns quickly under the impulse of the Spirit which drove me to express my daily encounters—and those of the Brothers—with the poor and with Christ. Grace typed and edited most of these stories and formulated an organized presentation of the entries in this book. I owe particular gratitude to Judith Allen who spent many hours in helping us to select what entries ought to be in the book.

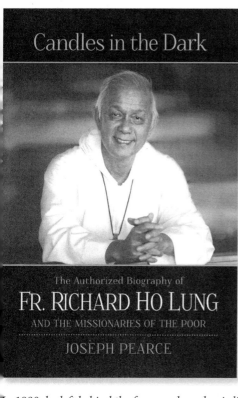

THE MISSIONARIES OF THE POOR (MOP) take vows of poverty, chastity, obedience and free service to the poorest of the poor.

Father Ho Lung and the MOP priests and brothers surrender all rights to their own material possessions, bodily desires, will and remuneration for services rendered to the poor. They have no private possessions and no bank accounts. The MOP live in community, sharing all things in common.

The material needs of the MOP are supplied by the generosity of readers like you—readers who share their faith, embrace their mission and offer their own resources to serve the poor.

To learn how you can assist the MOP in their mission and join them in serving the poor, visit their website at www.missionariesofthepoor.org. Or contact them at:

MISSIONARIES OF THE POOR, USA
P.O. Box 29893, Atlanta GA 30359
(404)-248-1197
E-mail: mopusaoffice@missionariesofthepoor.org
Contact Person: Jane Rodgers, MOP Asso.

MISSIONARIES OF THE POOR, JAMAICA
P.O. Box 8525
3 North Street, Kingston C.S.O.
(876)-948-0280/(876)-967-0341
E-mail: mopja@missionariesofthepoor.org
Contact Person: Bro. Praful Barla, MOP.

MISSIONARIES OF THE POOR, CANADA
P.O. Box 20070 Southbrook PO
Maple, Ontario L6A 4K0, Canada
(905)-940-2606
E-mail: mopcanada@gmail.com
Contact person: Sera Rossi, MOP Asso.